What people are saying about

Faerie Stones

A fascinating look into the world of faeries, stones and crystals; relating a wide variety of mythologies and traditions about nature spirits as well as containing comprehensive illustrated guides to a wide variety of stones and crystals plus meditation exercises for readers to try themselves. Another very useful and highly informative book from author, Ceri Norman, *Faerie Stones* is perfect for anyone interested in working with nature spirits, stones and crystals.

June Kent, Editor, Indie Shaman magazine

Ceri Norman has been a regular contributor to FAE Magazine for over ten years. Sharing her knowledge and insights of folklore and the faerie world, Ceri amazes us yet again with *Faerie Stones*. You will be hard pressed to find a more in-depth body of work looking at the many and varied crstals and stones associated with the faerie world. Authentic and well researched, *Faerie Stones* will satisfy your hunger for knowledge within the mineral realms of faerie.

Karen Kay, Editor in Chief, FAE Magazine

If you like to work with crystals and want to explore their connection to the world of Faerie then this is the book for you. Ceri explains how to work with the best Faerie stones and shares fascinating information on each one. The book also includes working with Faerie stones for your chakras and aura. Well written and extremely well researched.

Rachel Patterson, author of several books on The Craft including *Moon Magic, Kitchen Witchcraft* and *The Cailleach*

Faerie Stones

An Exploration of the Folklore
and Faeries Associated with
Stones and Crystals

Faerie Stones

An Exploration of the Folklore
and Faeries Associated with
Stones and Crystals

Ceri Norman

MOON
BOOKS

Winchester, UK
Washington, USA

First published by Moon Books, 2018
Moon Books is an imprint of John Hunt Publishing Ltd., Laurel House, Station Approach,
Alresford, Hants, SO24 9JH, UK
office1@jhpbooks.net
www.johnhuntpublishing.com
www.moon-books.net

For distributor details and how to order please visit the 'Ordering' section on our website.

Text copyright: Ceri Norman 2017

ISBN: 978 1 78535 719 0
978 1 78535 720 6 (ebook)
Library of Congress Control Number: 2017936847

A CIP catalogue record for this book is available from the British Library.

Design: Stuart Davies

Printed and bound by CPI Group (UK) Ltd, Croydon, CR0 4YY, UK

We operate a distinctive and ethical publishing philosophy in
all areas of our business, from our global network of authors to
production and worldwide distribution.

Contents

Introduction

That we find a crystal or a poppy beautiful means we are less alone,
that we are more deeply inserted into existence than the course of a
single life would lead us to believe.[1]
John Berger

Stones attract Faeries. They are as drawn to them and their
properties as we are. They may make their homes in stones,
use them for healing or simply play or be with them, enjoying
their beauty and energies. Faeries understand their rock-people
kin and have a wonderful working relationship with them. We
can learn from this relationship and from Faerie stories to build
and develop our own relationship with Faeries and stones. This
relationship is quite literally as old as the hills and has been
acknowledged through the ages. One old Anglo-Saxon name was
Aelfstan meaning 'Elf-Stone'[2] and countless stones are known as
Fairy Stones, Fairy Crosses, Elf Stones and the like.

Fairies love stones as they love the Earth and all who dwell
upon it. They are not as fussy as humans for they love all stones,
minerals, rocks and crystals, from the sparkly and shiny Fairy
Diamond to the rough, rugged Holed Stones found on beaches
and riverbeds, and from the tiniest of granular Quartz crystals
to entire mountains of Granite. Just as every tree has its Dryad,
every spring its Naiad, and every glen its Alseid, every stone
has its own Faerie. No matter how it looks, no matter how big
or small it may be, each stone has its own inner spirit or Faerie
with its own personality and its own wisdom to share. There are
even whole races of Faeries and spirits who live in and watch
over rocks and stones such as the Frideans of Scotland and the
Ngen-kura of South America.

Faeries are very practical as well as magical in all their
workings and do not require us to have a vast collection of

precious or semi-precious gemstones in order to work with them; they remind us that all stones are magical and precious in their own unique way so all you really need is a stone – a gemstone, tumblestone or pebble that speaks to you.

Healing with crystals and minerals, or working with them in ritual, is so ancient a concept that it is likely that modern humans, or *homo sapiens* to give us our scientific name, were not even the first human species to do it. There's evidence that Neanderthals were using Red Ochre in funerary rites from about 250,000 years ago, perhaps to help prepare the deceased for their rebirth into the Otherworld after death[3]. Mineral pigments were also used for thousands of years to create imaginative and ritual rock art from the Lascaux caves of France to Kakadu National Park in Australia. Rock art made with minerals shows us that our ancestors considered themselves a part of nature and the natural world rather than above it, and this is something the Faeries and the stones of the world are keen to remind us of. By working with stones we can get back to nature and commune with the Rock People and the Faeries who are our kin for we are all born of this universe and of this planet. Just as the Faerie Path, Paganism and other nature-based paths are enjoying a resurgence in the New Age so too is the modality of Crystal Healing.

Faeries are well known for hoarding precious metals, gemstones and anything else that takes their fancy. Faeries and stones are intrinsically linked in folklore and legend from the Gold-loving Leprechaun to the Icelandic Elves who inhabit boulders and exert their revenge on any human foolish enough to mess with their home stone. Many rock formations are rumoured to be Trolls or Faeries who danced on the Sabbath or who stayed out too late and were petrified by the Sun. Many natural rock formations as well as stone circles, cairns and other megalithic sites were allegedly created by Faeries and their kin, such as Elva Plain Stone Circle in Cumbria, which local legends say was built by Elves and Imps[4], the Giant's Causeway was allegedly created by the Faerie hero Fionn mac Cumhaill and the passage grave of Barclodiad Y Gawres on Anglesey was created from rocks that fell from the apron of the Giantess and Faerie Goddess of Winter, The Cailleach[5]. Countless other rocky places and ancient stone monuments are reputed to be Faerie homes or haunts, like the souterrain in Cornwall known as the Fairy's Fogou or Piskey's Hall, Puck Church Parlour cave in a cliff in East Sussex or the Mermaid's Chair rock feature in Mill Bay on Stronsay.

Stone circles, like Faerie Rings, have long been viewed as gateways or portals into Faerieland and places we can go to in order to speak with the Faeries. Isobel Gowdie, the seventeenth century witch of Auldearn, in Scotland, mentioned meeting with the Queen of Faerie at the nearby Auldearn Stone Circle and of being entertained by the Faerie Queen in her home beneath the hollow hills as part of her confessions.

Even ancient single standing stones may be known as Fairy Stones and often have local legends and characters attached to them like the Fairy Stones in Macclesfield and Allithwaite, the Pixie Stone in Chagford, Glac an T-Sìth ('Stone of the Faeries') in Inverness-shire, Creag na Fear Beag ('Stone of the Little Men') on Ben Loyal, Clach na Sithean ('Stone of the Fairies') near Grandtully – said to have been shaped by the Faeries sharpening their knives upon it[6], Carreg Y Bwci ('Stone of the Pwca/Goblin') in Carmarthenshire, La Eoque Des Faies (Stone of the Fairies) near Le Bourg de la Foret on Guernsey[7] and the several La Pierre/La Roche des Fées ('Stone/Rock of the Fairies') in France.

Faeries are well known to inhabit old stone buildings with castles and manor houses being a firm favourite. Herstmonceux Castle is home to a Goblin who guards a treasure chest[8]; in Spenser's *Faerie Queene* there is a mention of a hollow cave inhabited by Sprites below Dynevor Castle; Hylton Castle was home to a very mischievous Brownie known as the Cauld Lad o' Hylton; both Castle Howe and Barlow Castle are inhabited by Faeries. It is not just castles on land either, the Morgens, the Mermaid-like beings of Cornwall, Wales and Brittany, live in castles of Gold or crystal beneath the waves[9].

Many Faerie Monarchs are said to live in castles made of crystal. Arianrhod (possibly the Argante of Arthurian Lore) inhabits a sparkling, crystalline spiral castle. Some say this is the Corona Borealis or Northern Crown constellation in the northern sky, while others say that Arianrhod's crystal castle lies beneath or above Glastonbury Tor or at the aptly named Caer Arianrhod reef off the coast of Gwynedd. The crystal castle of Gwynn ap Nudd, a Welsh Faerie King who is featured in Arthuriana, is also said to lie either beneath Glastonbury Tor as stated in the Legend of St Collen, or is at *Caer Drewyn* – 'Gwyn's Fort' in Clwyd. Clíodhna, an Irish Goddess and the Queen of the Banshees, was reputed to have her palace in the heart of a pile of rocks, known by the name of Carrig-Cleena, near Mallow in County Cork.

Certain Faeries are said to live in our homes alongside us, such as Brownies and Kobolds, and by working with stones and the concept of Faerie space we can make them feel as at home in our homes as we are. Other Faeries prefer to live in our out buildings, such as barns and greenhouses, or in our gardens or fields. One wise old piece of advice states: *'A heap of stones in a field should not be disturbed... The fairies are said to live inside the pile and to move the stones would be most unfortunate.'*[10]

Stones and items made from stone or earthenware have long been used to provide offerings to Faeries. Household Brownies are particularly fond of receiving their bread and milk in earthenware dishes and in the Highlands libations of milk would be poured onto stones with specially hollowed-out tops as thanks for the local Faeries for watching over the cattle. Several of these stones can be still be visited today, including Clach na Glaisteg ('Stone of the Glaisteg' – beautiful half-women half-goat beings that tended cattle) and Clach na Gruagach

('Stone of the Gruagach' – female Brownies who often acted as dairymaids), both in Argyll and Bute.

Minerals and gemstones, those prized by humans in times past, are rich in folklore and legend. Specific crystals have been attributed with all sorts of healing, magical and protective powers from the outrageous to the surprisingly practical. Crystal 'remedies' appear in Ancient Egyptian texts such as the Ebers Papyrus, in the Vedas of Ancient India and in old Anglo-Saxon charms. Certain minerals have also found their way into modern medicines, such as Lithium, which is used for treating bipolar disorder.

There are countless legends of healing stones from all over the world. One of the best known concerns Mên-an-Tol in Cornwall[11], which is best known for its holed central stone. Mên-an-Tol is reputedly home to a very lovely Fairy or Pixie who loves to perform miraculous cures. Crawling through the hole was thought to make a person whole and well again and people with all sorts of ailments, such as rheumatism, rickets and asthma, have passed through it over the years in the hope of it bringing some Faerie and stone healing. In one old story, a changeling baby was put through the holed stone in order for the mother to get the real child back. Evil Pixies had changed her child, but the ancient stones were able to reverse their evil spell.

There are also examples of more portable healing stones in a whole array of colours. St Columba was associated with several healing stones. Some Anglo-Saxons seem to have worn clear crystal balls set in silver that were placed in water to imbue the water with healing properties[12]. Such healing stones seem to have been collected mostly for their colour. White stones were very popular for general healing work and were considered so Faerie that many builders refused to work with white stones for fear of upsetting the Faeries. Red stones were also popular: the *Clach Dearg* ('Red Stone') added healing energy to water and was used by St Columba to banish demons[13], while the power of the *Fuil*

Siochare ('Faerie Blood Stones') was said to come from that fact that they were the solidified blood of Faeries. There's also tell of a magical blue stone that always remained wet to the touch, blue is after all the colour associated with water, which was used to procure favourable winds for fishermen, heal stitches and which also had oaths sworn upon it[14]. Green has always been considered a healing colour, so it is no surprise that there's also mention of a green stone known as *Clach Leigh* (the 'Medicine Stone') that was reputed to cure just about every ailment known to man or beast[15]. Black stones were used to draw off pain, as if they are expected to absorb the pain in the same way that they absorb light[16].

Many churches have had healing stones built into their altars and there is mention in *The Book of Exodus* of the twelve stones upon the breastplate of the High Priest that represent the Twelve Tribes of Israel. It is also theorised that the use of different stones from different parts of Orkney to build the Ring of Brodgar was also done to symbolise the different communities or families on the islands and bring them together. In the same way stones can be used to represent places with which you may be – or wish to be – connected or to represent or connect you to certain types of Faeries or Faerie Monarchs with whom that crystal or stone is associated.

The Faeries have been known to gift stones to those they wish to connect to; these are very precious gifts and to be treasured. Many of these have been said to enable the lucky human to see or hear Faeries or to bring them good fortune. The Scottish Seer Coinneach Odhar was gifted one such Holed Stone by the Faeries after sleeping on a Fairy Mound[17]. The stone enabled him to not only see Faeries, but also to make prophecies. Such stones are still passed down in some families and magical lineages. In some tales Faeries drink from Golden goblets adorned with gemstones[18], one of which was probably Amethyst. Faerie gems, usually set in rings, were often gifted in legends to render the wearer invisible so that they might defeat monsters[19] or to cast a Faerie glamour on the wearer. It is feasible that the gemstone was in fact the Faerie in disguise and shows how intricately Faeries and stones are linked. In Shakespeare's *Romeo and Juliet* mention is made of Queen Mab being *'In shape no bigger than an agate-stone on the forefinger of an alderman.'*[20]

Certain stones were considered so special or valuable that they were traded or carried vast distances over the ancient world. Classic examples of this are the pieces of Baltic Amber that ended up in Ancient Egyptian tombs or the Ancient Britons dragging massive lumps of Preseli Bluestone more than 150 miles from South Wales to Wiltshire.

Several stones in myth and legend bear the name 'The Stone of Destiny'. There is the Stone of Jacob, the stone pillow on which Jacob rested his head when he had the vision of the ladder from Earth up to Heaven as described in *The Book of Genesis*, showing us how powerful dreaming and vision work with stones can be. Another is the *Pedra Fadada* (Spanish for 'The Stone of Destiny') that Goídel Glas, ancestor of the Gaels, chose as his seat in Spain. Most famous has to be the Stone of Scone, also called The Stone of Destiny or The Coronation Stone. Made of Red Sandstone, it was used in the coronation of the monarchs of Scotland, and later the monarchs of England and Great Britain. Some say that the Stone of Scone is also the Irish Stone of Destiny, the Lia Fáil, but others consider them to be separate stones. This is the stone of most interest to those who wish to work with the Fae as it is one of the four great magical treasures, or jewels, brought to Ireland by the Sidhe or Tuatha Dé Danann who are the Faerie race of Ireland. The Lia Fáil was used as the coronation stone for the High Kings of Ireland. When the rightful king sat upon it, it roared with joy and like many other magical stones it had to power to energise and rejuvenate the rightful king, enabling him to have a long reign. *Lia Fáil* literally means 'Stone of Ireland'. These stones all confer power, for stones have power in and of themselves as well as the powers that we ascribe to them. Anyone kissing the Blarney Stone is said to be awarded the gift of the gab, in other words the ability to be very flattering, coaxing and clever with words. Other stones are credited with the ability to discern if someone is lying or telling the truth, such as the *Cloch Labhrais* or 'Answering Stone' near Stradbally in Ireland.

There are many ways to work with Faeries and stones. We can wear stone jewellery, carry stones in our pockets or handbags, or place them in and around our home, garden, workspace and car. We can place them on our altars or bedside tables. We can meditate with them, journey into them or with them, dream with them or make magic with them. They can teach us so many things about ourselves and the world in which we live. They can help us to heal or to heal ourselves, give us guidance, protect us and support us. Specific stones can connect us to specific energies, they can calm us, enliven us or help us to focus. Certain stones connect us to certain Faerie Monarchs and Faerie beings with whom we can forge friendships and lasting bonds and stones are magical portals into all things Faerie. We can work with Faeries and stones to create sacred space by gridding or laying out our own stone circles or even for divination by casting stones like the shamans of old.

It is my hope that you will develop and deepen your relationship with the Faeries by working with stones and the Faeries who dwell therein. You may even find the Faeries gifting you with stones and Stone Faeries that they feel may help you on your path. What follows are a few Faerie favourites. If you explore the mineral realm for yourselves, you will find many more...

A Note on the Use of Elements
The numbers and types of elements used in the world today vary enormously. The Periodic Table has 118 elements of which only the first 94 elements occur in nature, numbers 95 to 118 have

been synthesised by mankind. Both the Ancient European and Asian systems have five elements each, although these differ: for Europe it is Earth, Air, Fire, Water and Spirit while in Asia it is Wood, Metal, Fire, Water and Earth. The Faerie Star with its seven points is linked with seven Faerie elements of Earth, Air, Fire, Water, Above/Cosmos, Below/Deep Earth and Within/ Spirit. I've tried to work with a system that truly represents the elements that stones are linked with and these go beyond the old systems and have utilised the ancient systems and then added several more elements that are helpful. Ice is neither quite Water nor Earth, but somewhere between as it is solidified water and this is what the ancients thought Clear Quartz was. Nature incorporates more life than either Wood or Earth and Magic really is its own element.

Part One: Looking For and Looking After Stones

Geologists have a saying – rocks remember.
Neil Armstrong

Whenever possible it is always best to seek out stones that have been ethically collected with relevant permissions by well-paid workers who care about crystals. Some stones are hand gathered from outcrops, but unfortunately most stones and crystals today have been mined unethically and traumatised by being blasted or ripped from Mother Earth. We too have suffered traumas in our life and if a stone comes into your life that has been traumatised in this way, you can help it heal just as crystals are thought to help us to benefit from their metaphysical properties. In fact, this shared trauma can sometimes help you to bond and befriend crystals. You can literally help them get their shine and power back with some serious tender loving care.

Many people like to collect pebbles from nature, but this is also unethical. The problem is that nowadays mankind thinks it owns everything, so taking a stone from a field or even the beach is technically theft unless you own the land or can obtain permission from the landowner. The ownership of English beaches is very complicated: the area above the high water mark belongs to whoever owns the adjacent land, but the area between the high water mark and the low water mark, and below the low water mark belongs to the Crown. Some beaches, such as Chesil Beach, are also Sites of Special Scientific Interest or World Heritage Sites. Hopefully it goes without saying, never, ever take stones from a sacred site or chip bits off one, no matter how much you feel connected to a place. There are countless tales of people who have taken stones from sacred sites only to be cursed with bad luck until they return the stone with a heartfelt apology. A very well known instance of this is Pele's Curse: the belief that taking rocks or stones from the Islands of Hawaii will invoke the anger of the local Volcano Goddess, Pele, who views all the rocks and stones as her children until those stone children are returned to her. In serious cases it has also believed that theft of and damage to stones has even resulted in death. The death of the Barber Surgeon of Avebury is one such case. The Barber Surgeon either sought to cart off one of the stones for building materials or destroy one of the stones to de-Paganise the site depending on the version, but by some very fast-acting Karma was promptly crushed to death beneath the very stone he was attempting to remove[21]. There is some truth to this legend as his skeleton was excavated in 1938, complete with his gear.

Stones choose us as much as we choose them; they come into our lives for a reason, although that reason is not always clear at the time. There are many ways to seek out stones and many ways in which they seek us out. If you're looking for help with a particular issue, or just looking for the most appropriate stone to be with you at that time, ask for the right stone to come and find you or reveal itself to you. Quite often a stone will catch your eye – you will find yourself very drawn to it. It may not be the biggest, the prettiest, the most colourful, or the shiniest, but be sure it has called out to you for a very good reason – it wants to work with you. If you are choosing from a selection of stones, for example in a New Age store, and nothing catches your eye, try sensing the stones and see if any give you 'vibes'. Place your hands over the stones or place them in your hand one at a time and feel what vibrations you pick up from the stones. You may find that one feels warmer or colder to the touch, or that gives you the tingles. These sensations can occur in your hand where the stone is or they can also occur in other parts of your body, for example as a warm feeling in your Heart Chakra area, as a pull in your gut – just like a gut feeling, or as a buzz in your brain area near either your Crown or Third Eye Chakras. If you feel any of these sensations then that stone is speaking to you and wishes to join you on your journey. If it is not possible to really see or touch a stone before purchasing or obtaining it, perhaps because it is from an online retailer, many of whom batch-sell rather than photographing every stone individually, you can still go with your feelings. Does the idea of the stone and its name as you see it on the web page give you good vibes? If so, know that the right stone for you is going to make its way to you. Stones can also be gifted to us by friends and family, again know that the stone has had something to do with that!

You will also get feelings and sensations when a particular stone from your collection is wishing to work with you at any time. That stone piece of jewellery that's been sitting in your drawer for a bit may suddenly catch your eye as if to say, 'Wear me!' Or you find yourself thinking, 'Yeah, I'd love to wear you today.' Those are great signs. ' As you cast your eyes over your collection, a stone may sparkle at you, catching the light just right, to say, 'Hello, please choose me today.' You can pass your hand over your stones and see which one or ones give you a warm or cold sensation, or you may randomly select it from your stone collection with your eyes closed. If you feel you would like to work with stones and their Faeries for help with working through or healing a certain issue, you can always ask them which one or ones can best assist you. They will be happy to let you know.

If you're new to energy working or for any reason don't find yourself getting strong sensations from the stones, you can try working with a pendulum as a go between twixt you and the stones. Pass your pendulum over the stones available to you. If you have a specific purpose in mind that you're looking for help with, tell the stones and the pendulum, otherwise simply ask whichever stone wishes to work with you at this time to reveal itself to you. Does the pendulum pull towards a certain stone or try to drop from your fingers over one? Does it start circling over a certain stone? These are all good indicators. You, the stones and their Faeries all know on some level what you need and which of them can best help you at any time, so trust them and trust your higher self to guide you.

Some stones will leave us once their mission with us is complete while others stay with us for our time on Earth. There are times when you will feel the need to gift one of your stones to another person, this is because the stone has completed its work with you and can now help that new person, just as they have helped you. If this happened, thank the stone for all its assistance and give it to its new caretaker with love. Some stones will magically become lost; this is often because the Faeries and stone have decided to move on either temporarily or permanently (although sometimes it can be a little bit of cheekiness from the Faeries). Sometimes these stones can turn up again, sometimes not. Be grateful for the time you had together and trust that whatever happens could well be meant to be. However, if your feelings tell you that it is down to mischievousness rather than the stone's natural time to move on from your life, you are quite entitled to ask the Faeries to return it or for the stone to find you again. Occasionally Faeries will require something in return, say a shiny stone or coin of their own to play with.

When a stone comes into your life, it will have already picked up many energies from where it was born, the cultures that developed in that area, where it has since been, how it was mined and from all the people who handled it before it reached you, such as miners, merchants and postal workers. Cleansing stones will not only rid the stones of these energies, it will also clear out any negative energies and allow the stone to rest and rejuvenate itself.

There are many different ways to cleanse and recharge stones. Some stones will definitely have one preferred method while others might like trying different methods. Amber, for example, with its fiery and earthy energy, loves both Earth cleansing and Sun bathing. Think of it like a human with the whole bath or shower preference thing; some of us love baths, some love showers and others will do whatever they feel like at that moment. You'll need to first consider what type of stone you are dealing with, salt-based stones and calcite will actually dissolve in water, so that's a definite no-no. Whichever method you choose, it is well worth cleansing and recharging your stones regularly to help keep them healthy, happy and free of any stagnant or negative energies. Think of it like their spa day! Stones and the Stone Faeries will generally tell you how they wish to be cleansed and recharged and how long for. Don't be afraid to ask the stone what it wants as it'll be only too pleased to let you know.

Moon Bathing

This involves leaving the stone below the light of the Full Moon, allowing it to soak up the silvery energies of the Moon overnight. Many people enhance this by placing the stones on a cloth of white or silver. The Full Moon is especially loved by Faeries who love to dance below it. You can do this outside in your garden (but be warned the Faeries may think it is a gift and run off with it) or inside on a window ledge. Moon bathing works very well for all non Sun-orientated stones, those that might fade in sunlight or focus the Sun's rays and for very delicate stones. Stones that adore this method include Moonstone, for which it is especially potent, all of the Fairy Quartz formations, Jet, Snow Quartz, Clear Quartz, Fluorite, Calcite Fairy Stones, Cassiterite, Amethyst and Aquamarine.

Sun Bathing

Some of your stones will be Sun lovers just as some humans are. Leaving your stones out on a window ledge on a sunny day can really enliven them. A cloth of gold, yellow or orange under the stones can enhance the Sun's energies. Do not use this method with any of the Quartzes as they can fade and even start fires! Stones that love bathing in sunshine include Amber, Carnelian, Garnet, Flint, Chiastolite Fairy Stones, Preseli Bluestone and Moss Agate.

Cleansing with Water

A very popular and easy to use method. Simply run the stone under running water or place it in a little pot of water for a while. Some combine this with Moon or Sun bathing. It is best to use water from natural sources such as a river or spring rather than tap water, which contains a lot of chemicals. Aquamarine and Holed Stones really love water cleansing. Do not use water with Calcite Fairy Stones.

Salt Cleansing

Placing your stone in salt can help draw off any stagnant energies, and salt itself is a crystal. Staurolite Fairy Cross Stones are very fond of this method.

Cluster or Geode Cleansing

Smaller stones can be cleansed and revitalised by placing them within a crystal Geode or on a crystal Cluster and they will pick up a little of the Cluster or Geode's energy in this way so you'll need to make sure that their energies are compatible. Remember that the Geode or Cluster will also need cleansing and recharging periodically. This works very well with Fairy Crystal formations and the Quartz family in general.

Smudging

Stones can be passed through incense smoke in order to be cleansed, but in my experience this method does not recharge stones very effectively, so is best used along with other methods.

Sound Cleansing

Stones can be cleansed with sound as stones and sound both work through vibrations. Make sure that whatever sound making tool you use has a pleasant tone. Play the tone close to your stones so that its sound carries through the stone, transmuting its energies. Sound making tools that you can use include bells, Tibetan singing bowls, drums, cymbals and even your stereo. Stones with a softness to them or a deep Earth origin, such as Calcite and Granite, adore this method of cleansing.

Intention or Visualisation

This method is the stone version of a quick shower or power nap. It involves 'seeing' or intending that the stone be cleansed and charged and works best as a stop-gap between deeper cleansing or energising sessions.

Earth Cleansing

By placing stones back into the Earth they can recharged from Mother Earth. This is a very powerful and potent method for those that were born of the Earth in any way. It is very easy to lose stones if you bury them directly back into the Earth as they may feel that they are going home and leave you or you may not remember quite where you put them. The best way to do this is to bury a brown glass jar into some soil, say in your garden or in a pot of soil, then place the stone inside the jar, pop the lid back on and leave for between one and three days, depending on the stone's needs. Stones that enjoy Earth cleansing include Moss Agate/Tree Agate and all the Quartzes.

Storage

Stones will also have their own ideas about how and where they would like to be kept when not in active use. Some, like Jet, appreciate being put safely away in wooden boxes, some like being wrapped in cloth, such as Amethyst and Fluorite, and some will detest the idea of being put away at all, instead preferring to be kept out in pride of place or on your Faerie Altar, including Calcite Faerie Stones, and some like to be placed near plants or other greenery, including Moss Agate and Aventurine. Again, every stone will have its own preferences and might even like to go exploring around your home until it finds its perfect new place.

Part Two: Faerie Stones

If it weren't for the rocks in its bed, the stream would have no song.[22]
Carl Perkins

Amber

Other Names: *Bernstein* ('Burn Stone' in German), *Jainitar* ('Sea-Resin' in Phoenician), Eolh ('Light of the Sun' in Anglo-Saxon), Electrum ('Brilliant Sun' in Latin), Glessum or Chryselectrum

Chemical Composition: $C_{10}H_{16}O$

Element: Fire and Earth

Season: Summer

Planet: The Sun

Chakra: Solar Plexus

Birthstone: Taurus and November

Other: National gemstone of Germany, Lithuania and Romania. Regional stone for East Anglia in the UK

Faerie Monarchs/Deities: All Sun-associated monarchs, e.g. Freyja, Thor, Áine, Brighid, Baldr, Lugh/Llew, Druantia, Jurate, Ra, Belenos, Amaterasu, Beiwe, Apollo and Saulė

Faeries: Dryads especially those of the pine tree, Elves, Tree Sprites, Nymphs, Alseids and Dwarves

Amber is an amazing substance that is millions of years old and therefore carries with it very ancient wisdom and magic. The Faeries that accompany Amber have lived through almost everything imaginable and can offer us guidance and comfort because of their great experience. Amber comes in many colours, most commonly ranging from bone-like white, through lemon-yellow, honey, cognac and cherry to almost black. Blue Amber and natural green Amber can also be found, although they are very rare.

Not technically a crystal, Amber is the fossilised resin of an ancient tree akin to the modern pine. As the resin was exuded from the tree and fell to the ground, Amber sometimes has picked up inclusions along the way. These inclusions can be anything from air bubbles to leaf litter or bark to insects and even feathers. Inclusions can be quite sought-after for their beauty or for their paleontological importance. The inclusions are indicative of life going on all around us even if we don't particularly notice it because we are focused on other things. Like us, the tree and its Amber do not exist in a vacuum, but in bustling, busy nature where we are surrounded by Faeries if we only stop, look and listen. Because it has an organic origin and comes from trees, Amber it is beloved by Dryads and Forest Elves who dwell within the forests and who care for the trees therein. Wearing jewellery of Amber or carrying some in your pocket can help you connect to the Dryads, Elves and Tree Spirits and their wisdom wherever you happen to be, even if it's in the midst of the concrete jungle.

Amber is said to hold the power of a thousand suns due to both its warm-hued appearance and the fact that as the tree that made the resin grew in the sunlight over many years it is said to have absorbed the power of the Sun over days and many long summers. It certainly has a very warming energy to it and, unlike crystals, Amber is warm to the touch and therefore highly tactile. In the ancient world Pliny, citing Nicias, wrote of how Amber was said to be, *'A liquid produced by the rays of the sun; and that these rays, at the moment of the sun's setting, striking with the greatest force upon the surface of the soil, leave upon it an unctuous sweat, which is carried off by the tides of the ocean, and thrown up upon the shores of Germany.'* It certainly has a very sunny disposition and like the pine torches of old, Amber brings inspiration and enlightenment and can help light our way. Amber was also known as Eolh in Anglo-Saxon[23], perhaps meaning something like 'light streaming forth from the Sun', and Eolh is also the Anglo-Saxon name for the Rune better known today as Algiz. Eolh refers to the Elk or the Elk-Sedge, a rather sharp type of marsh-loving plant. Eolh is a Rune of protection, especially Divine protection, and represents the concept of reaching for the stars or the Divine as the Rune itself looks rather like a man with his arms up reaching for the heavens. We too can reach up to the heavens, to the powerful Sun or out to the realm of the Fae to ask for protection, guidance, enlightenment and inspiration.

For some Amber represents the feminine Faeries, Faerie Queens and the Goddess. Many traditions have Goddesses of the Sun such as the Norse Goddess Freyja, whose name means 'Lady', thereby connecting her to the Lady of the Wiccan tradition. For others Amber represents the masculine Faeries, Faerie Kings and the Gods such as the golden-red bearded Thor and the solar aspects and light of Baldr and Llew/Lugh.

In many legends Amber is described as having been formed from the tears of deities and heroes. In Greek myth after Phaeton, the son of the Sun God Helios, was killed, his sisters became poplar tree or Dryads of poplars and their falling tears became Amber[24]. From Lithuania comes the tale of Jurate's tears. Jurate was the Queen of the Sea who fell in love with a humble fisherman. Her father, Perkunas, was enraged by this because he had already promised her to the God of Water, Patrimpas. Her father killed the fisherman, destroyed Jurate's Amber Palace – bits of which still wash up on Baltic shores, and transformed Jurate into sea foam[25]. When Freyja lost her husband Odr she searched the world for him and wept many tears; where her tears fell on land they became Gold and where they landed on water they became Amber. Freyja, who is the Faerie Queen of the Dís – Faerie Spirits who watched over particular families and homes – famously wore the necklace Brisingamen, crafted from Gold and Amber. It was made by four dwarves known as the Brisings. Freyja obtained the necklace in exchange for spending one night each with the four Brising Dwarves. This exchange emphasises that Amber's lesson is all about giving and receiving in balance. In the Old Norse Poem the *Hávamál* ('Sayings of the High One'), one of the sayings is, *'A gift in return for a gift.'* Another says, *'With presents friends should please each other... Mutual giving makes for friendship.'*[26] These beautifully sum up our connection with the Faeries: we leave out gifts and offerings for them in exchange for their friendship, blessings and magic.

Despite its links with grief, Amber is a sunny and bright material with a very positive upbeat energy that can inspire us and chase the blues away. It brings light to the darkness, in terms of positivity and in terms of creativity, as it can help us to connect with our Muse – a Faerie Queen and Greek Goddess of Inspiration. Amber is a great cleanser of negative energies from the human energy system and from our environment. Traditionally Amber is credited with curing just about anything and everything. In the Scandinavian and Baltic countries in particular wearing Amber is said to help ease the aches and pains of those with arthritis, ease colds and respiratory problems and generally promote good health and long life. With its sunny energy it is worn by many who live with SAD syndrome as part of their winter coping strategy along with using light lamps. As bracelets and anklets it can be worn by those who suffer from cold or pain at their extremities. Amber demonstrates to us how to heal ourselves with the help of the Dryads and Tree Spirits; after all the resin that became Amber was originally exuded from the tree as part of its own healing process when the tree was faced with trauma and injury of some kind. We too suffer traumas and injury in our lives and can learn to heal ourselves over time.

Sometimes Amber from the Baltic washes up on the coasts of Eastern England. It is considered very good luck to find some. Amber beads have long been worn for protection, especially by children. In the past children were given Amber bead necklaces to protect them from witchcraft and malevolent Faeries. Nowadays children are given such necklaces to help them with the aches and pains of teething. Here Amber reminds us of both the protective and malevolent nature of Fae, because while some Faeries love to help us protect our little ones from harm, others seek to swap human babies for changelings...

Amber has long been held sacred and used for good luck charms, magical talismans and in magical practices since at least 30,000 years ago. Amber was used to make spindle whorls from Syria to Scandinavia because of its electrostatic properties, which must have seemed positively magical to our ancestors. Due to its softness, Amber is easy to carve and form into various shapes. Amulets in the shapes of animals – perhaps for totemic reasons, deities – usually Goddesses/Faerie Queens, lunar symbols and solar symbols have been found.

Amber was very popular in both the Viking/Norse and Celtic cultures and Amber items, especially beads, are often found as grave goods. Many of these beads and carvings such as those in the collection of carved Amber objects in the J. Paul Getty Museum, show clear signs of use, suggesting they were adored and used for adornment for long periods before being buried with their owners so that their owners could continue to have them in the afterlife. The link between Amber and grief, the fact that certain amulets appear to have not been used before being buried with the dead and references like that found in *The Fall of Troy* where golden Amber objects were laid out with Ajax's body at his funeral[27], suggests that Amber was also of great importance in funerary rites. Amber could also be given as a coming of age gift, or to signify a change in status or state of being: a necklace of Amber or 'Lammer' beads was once a traditional gift from a mother to her daughter upon her wedding day in parts of Scotland[28]. The use of Amber at the crossing over times of being single to being married and for the journey from this life to the next shows how Amber was used to ensure safe passage when passing between realms or stages of life. Wearing or holding Amber can be protective for any form of journeying, whether in terms of dreams, meditations or magically crossing over between our world and the world of the Faeries or for more mundane journeys by car, plane or boat. Indeed ancient Vikings and Scots sailors used to carry Gold coins or pieces of Amber that they would throw overboard as offerings to placate angry Sea Deities or Sea Sprites.

Although her name suggests a strong link with the oak tree (the old Celtic words for 'oak' being *derw* or *deru*), the Gallic Goddess and tree protectress Druantia, also known as 'The Queen of the Druids' is closely associated with pine trees[29]. In the Celtic Tree Calendar and Ogham writing system, Amber, due to its pine origins, is representative of Ailim, referring to the pine tree or fir. Pine is particularly loved by its local Land-Wights, who are Faeries of a specific locale, and by Dwarves[30]. As pine is one of the tallest growing trees, Ailim is all about getting an overview on things, looking at things from a new perspective and considering the perspectives of others. Like Ailim and the pine, the Faeries often encourage us to look at things with new or childlike eyes to see the magic and wonder of the world around us. Amber encourages us to go out into the pine forests for ourselves to connect with Druantia and the Dryads and Spirits of the pine trees that we find there. It invites us to exchange energy and wisdom with those trees, perhaps by tree hugging or simply by taking the tree some water or clearing up any rubbish you find. There, within those ancient forests, can we find the beginnings of the answers to our questions, as represented by Ailim in the Word Ogham of Mac ind Óc, and there, like the Druids of old, we can be initiated into the mysteries of Amber, the ancient forests, the Dryads of the Forest and the Alseids – the Nymphs of the Groves.

Amethyst

Other Names: Lavendine or Bishop's Stone

Chemical Composition: SiO_2 The purple colour comes from the inclusion of Manganese (Mn) and Iron (Fe^{4+})

Element: Spirit and Magic

Season: The seasons of Faerieland, which do not necessarily tie in with our own

Planet: None as Amethyst instead relates to Avalon and the Realm of the Faeries

Chakra: Third Eye and Crown Chakras

Birthstone: Pisces, Aquarius and February

Anniversary: The sixth wedding anniversary

Other: Day Stone for Wednesdays. Amethyst is the official state gemstone of South Carolina, National Stone of Uruguay and a county gemstone for Cornwall

Faerie Monarchs/Deities: Morgan le Fay, Modron and Morgan Tud

Faeries: All Faeries, especially those skilled in the magical arts

Amethyst varies enormously in colour and in depth of hue, from the lightest pale violets and lavenders through to rich, deep purple. Sometimes it can lean more towards the red end of purple and other times more towards the blue. Generally speaking, the darker the colour, the more intense the energies are, while paler forms are far more soft and gentle. There may be inclusions of clear or white quartz and when bands of Snow/Clear Quartz and Amethyst form chevron shapes this is called Chevron Amethyst.

Traditionally Amethyst has been worn to assist in the management of migraines and headaches, insomnia and bad dreams as it calms the mind and clears the Third Eye Chakra. It has also been used to ease addictions, pain and depression.

It is credited with balancing our hormones and soothing bruising, whether that be physical bruising or bruised pride, and promoting healing of the skin.

Gentle yet powerful, protective amulets of Amethyst have been popular for centuries. Amethyst was popular in both Ancient Greece and Rome. In Britain, due to its purple colouring, it was linked to the notion of royal purple. There are several large and stunning quality Amethysts in Britain's Crown Jewels, especially in the coronation centrepieces of St Edward's Crown, the Sovereign's Orb and the Sovereign's Sceptre. Queen Elizabeth I also had an Amethyst necklace that she was particularly fond of. These very regal association highlight to us that Amethyst, as such a royal stone, can be used to communicate and connect to the Faerie Monarchs as all kings and queens seem to adore Amethyst.

The name Amethyst derives comes from the Ancient Greek *ά a-* ('not') and *μέθυστος méthystos* ('intoxicated'), referring to the traditional, if somewhat odd, belief that Amethyst protected its owner from getting drunk – don't try that at home! Not only did the Ancient Greeks wear a lot of Amethyst for this reason, they even made gorgeous drinking vessels from Amethyst. In this link with the consumption of that which makes us merry, Amethyst ties in with intoxicating and mesmerising revels of the Faeries, which many an unsuspecting human has witnessed and even been enchanted into. Faeries like to party and they love to remind us to have fun and celebrate life to the full. There is also a serious, deep and intense side to Amethyst that underlines the fact that we are only welcome at Faerie revels if we respect their rules and do not overstay our welcome, as many mortals have done in the past.

Amethyst really is the crystal par excellence of the Faerie Spiritual Path, or Fairy Faith as it was once known, as Amethyst has long been associated with the Divine in many forms, with Faeries and with magic, wisdom and intuition. It is not just the Fairy Faith that has strong links with Amethyst, in Tibet Amethyst is sacred to the Buddha. One of its nicknames is 'The Bishop's Stone' as Catholic Bishops and Archbishops often wear Episcopal rings set with a single Amethyst – perhaps so they do not get too intoxicated on communion wine. Beads of Amethyst have also been found as Anglo-Saxon grave goods in England[31].

For those of us on the Faerie Path, Amethyst and the Faeries who accompany Amethyst are very big on Faerie magic, spirituality and protection. They will guide you to become more aware of the Faeries all around you, help you to learn more of their magic and to hone your own magical and psychic abilities such as *clairvoyance* – 'clear seeing', *clairsentience* – 'clear feeling', *clairaudience* – 'clear hearing', and *claircognisance* – 'clear knowing'. By working on these four 'clairs', as they are known, we can learn to communicate more effectively with the Fae and to pick up more easily and clearly on their messages for us. Amethyst enhances positive magic and it is wonderful to work within a Faerie Star created by seven Amethyst crystals when working magic with Faeries. Many people also like to have an Amethyst or two to hand when performing any kind of divination, especially with any Faerie related oracles or Tarot decks; partly for spiritual protection and partly to increase the sensitivity of their 'clair' skills in order to enhance the reading. When not using your divination tools, keeping an Amethyst with them can help protect them from any negative energies.

Amethyst is very much the gemstone of the sorceress, shape-shifter, healer and Faerie Queen Morgan le Fay and the lilac mists, the lilac veil between worlds, that separate Glastonbury from Avalon in folklore. Morgan's family tree varies from tale to tale. In older versions she is the daughter of Avallach, King of Avalon and one of nine sisters skilled in healing arts who dwell in Avalon. In other, better known versions, Morgan is King Arthur's half-sister through their mother Ygraine. Morgan and Arthur have a strained relationship; in some legends Arthur and

Morgan get together despite the fact that they are half-siblings and Mordred, who was born from their union, ultimately kills his father. Eventually Arthur and Morgan do reconcile and Morgan takes Arthur to Avalon to be healed, where he will wait as the Once and Future King for when Britain again needs him to come to its aid.

Morgan's origins are truly ancient; she is connected to the Ancient Celtic Mother Goddess, Modron, and her name *Morgan* – 'Sea Born' in Welsh and Breton. This connects her to the Morgens or Morgans, who were Water Sprites or Spirits that lived in crystal castles beneath the waves. Her strong Faerie links are further evidenced by her epithet of le Fay, so her name means 'Morgan the Faerie'. In the earlier tales Morgan was literally a magical Faerie, but in later ones she is more human, though she is still said to have learned her magical arts from the Faeries. A similar, though male version, of Morgan called Morgan Tud can also be found in Arthurian lore. Here Morgan is the chief physician of King Arthur. Again the Morgan refers to the Sea Sprites and the epithet *Tud* means something like 'Sinister Faerie'[32].

Whether you prefer to work with Morgan le Fay or Morgan Tud, you can call on Morgan as an ally in your healing and magical work by asking Amethyst and its resident Faerie to act as an intermediary, especially as Amethyst is said to help remove toxins from the body, boost the immune system and generally help us to heal ourselves. It is a wonderful stone to use for meditation or to work with if you are facing bouts of insomnia, as it dispels fear and anxiety and promotes a sense of calm and of feeling safe. Amethyst is also traditionally used to facilitate clear mindedness.

Amethyst is a stone of the mysteries and of fate. Fate derives from the same word as Fae. The Fates, also called the Norns, were Faerie-like supernatural beings who controlled the destiny of mortals and of the Gods. We can meditate with Amethyst and call on the Fates, the Norns and Faeries if we seek to change our destinies or to find our purpose in life.

Amethyst is great to have on your Faerie altar to welcome in the Faeries, to focus that Faerie energy that can otherwise get a bit chaotic or airy-fairy, and to shield your altar from some of the more harmful energies found in our environment today, helping your altar to maintain its Otherworldly energies and sacredness. Wearing Amethyst signifies to the Faeries that you are open to working with them and learning their special magics. It can also be used in your home, especially by computers, to prevent the build up of geopathic stress or electro-magnetic energies. Amethyst is believed by crystal workers to literally be able to transmute negative energy into positive energy and shows us how to turn the negatives into positives. Meditating with Amethyst gives easy access to Avalon and the Faerie Otherworld as it parts the veils smoothly and safely.

Amethyst fades in bright sunlight, so be careful where you place it. Should you find the energy of Amethyst a little overwhelming, Fluorite is a gentle alternative.

Aquamarine

Other Names: Blue Beryl, Cyan Beryl or Chrysolite, or in its darkest blue form it's called Maxixe

Chemical Composition: $Be_3Al_2(Si_6O_{18})$. The pale blue colour of aquamarine is attributed to Iron (Fe^{2+})

Element: Water

Season: Spring with spring rains, summer and autumn

Planet: Earth and Venus

Chakra: Throat and Heart

Birthstone: Pisces, Scorpio, Cancer, October and March

Anniversary: The nineteenth wedding anniversary

Other: State Gemstone of Colorado

Faerie Monarchs/Deities: All those linked with rivers, oceans and other bodies of water like the Lady of the Lake, Sabrina, Danu, Arnemetia, Boann, Sulis Minerva, Sequana, Clota, Coventina, Saraswati, Mither O' the Sea, Nehalennia, Sedna, Anuket, Vellamo, Sirara, Rán, Njord and Manannan

Faeries: The Morgens, Mermaids and Merman, Fossegrim and Nix, Naiads, Oceanids, Nereids, Undines, Mami Wata, Sea Sprites and Selkies

Aquamarine is the blue or cyan form of Beryl. The name Aquamarine derives from the Latin *aqua marina*, meaning 'water of the sea' and with this watery aspect it accentuates the peace and power of the oceans and of our own ocean of emotions, which we are always trying to navigate. It is an ideal stone for those born under the watery astrological signs. Just like water, Aquamarine can cleanse away negative vibrations, negative emotions, negative thoughts about ourselves and others and our fears or anything else that may be holding us back. Aquamarine has the energy of the ocean on a summer's day, when there is gentle movement in the waters, rather than anything too tempestuous. That said though, even the soft gentle action of the waves has enormous power and can erode away hard rock as well as stubborn blockages.

Just like a shower or bath, the energy of Aquamarine and its Mermaid-Faerie guardians cleanses our minds, bodies and souls. Aquamarine is lovely and gentle to use to cleanse our Chakras, Aura and our energy systems as well as to cleanse the space in which we live. It gives the sense of a peaceful, cleansing, balancing walk by the sea. That's part of what the Guardians of Aquamarine's mission is all about, getting us out to the seaside, or by a river or lake, or to drink more water to engage with the energy of water, because not only is water vital to our own wellbeing it is vital to that of the planet as well. The Faerie Beings of the Waters, the Lady of the Lake, the Goddesses for whom rivers were named, the Morgens, the Mer-People, the Oceanids of the Oceans, the Sprites of Sea Spray and the Naiads of Streams, all want us to see what's going on with the state of our waterways and to do our bit for conservation, not just for their sakes, but also for the sakes of all water-dwelling creatures and for the sake of our own souls too. They want us to recycle more, to be careful what detergents we use that end up in the oceans, and they want us to be more vocal about marine conservation. Essentially they want mankind to stop treating the waterways like rubbish dumps. It is not a comfortable message for many who would rather ignore these serious global problems, but it is the truth and Aquamarine is very much about speaking our truth and finding our own truth.

Many Water Faeries are also linked with healing, as stated under Amethyst. Morgan Tud or Morgan le Fay was a renowned Faerie Healer and Physician, and the *Gwragedd Annwn* – 'Watery Woman of the Otherworld' of Llyn Y Fan Fach taught her healing knowledge to her sons who became the famous Physicians of Myddfai[33].

Many of our rivers, holy wells and waterways are named for Goddesses, Faerie Queens and Faeries. Many people still visit these wells and springs in the hope of healing. In Scotland and Ireland there are literally hundreds of wells named for St Bridget, healer, Irish Saint and Celtic Faerie Queen/Goddess of both Fire and Water. There's even a Roman-British inscription to Bridget as a Water Nymph – *Dea Nympha Brigantia*. The river Clyde is named for the Celtic Goddess Clota/Clud/Clwyd, the Danube for Danu and the Severn for Sabrina or Hafren, the Boyne for Boann, the Seine for the Gaulish Goddess Sequana and the Sarasvati River in India and Pakistan is named after the Hindu Goddess Saraswati. The Roman Baths at Bath were sacred to Sulis Minerva and the springs at Buxton are sacred to Arnemetia. There are also many Sea Goddesses: Nehalennia is often considered the Goddess of the North Sea, Rán was the Norse Sea Goddess, the Mither (Mother) of the Sea rules over the waves around Orkney, Sirara is the Sumerian Goddess of the Persian Gulf, and Sedna is the Inuit Goddess of the Arctic Seas around Greenland and Canada. There are many Fairy wells and Pixie wells all over the UK, many with their own resident Faerie who may grant wishes in exchange for suitable offerings such as at the Fairy Well near Maiden Castle, where local maidens would drop silver pins into the water to gain the Faeries' blessing. Just like these magical wishing wells, working with Aquamarine helps us to have our wishes granted as it helps us to manifest our wishes or improvements to circumstances or just a more positive attitude. Mermaids have also been known to grant wishes, although many people know them better as being more siren-like, luring sailors to their deaths. Truth be told, if you look carefully into those stories you will often find that how the Mermaid treats the human does depend on how the human treated the Mermaid in the first place. For example, Lutey treats the Mermaid of Lizard Point in Cornwall well and is rewarded with wishes[34], but woe betide anyone who chases or mistreats a Mermaid. In this way

Aquamarine highlights to us of the tide of Karma, that what we do to others comes back to us. In this Aquamarine and its associated Faerie Monarchs and Elementals really would rather that we worked on our compassion, understanding and love ourselves so that Karma doesn't have to come and bite us.

There are also many Faerie Kings associated with Water. Njord is the Norse God of the Sea, the Winds and of Abundance. His love for the sea was absolute and was a big part of why his marriage to the Snow Goddess Skadi did not work out as she loved her snowy mountains and could not stand the sea, while he loved the sea and couldn't stand the mountains. Njord is a very kindly and very deep Faerie King to work with, especially in manifestation magic and marine conservation. Manannán mac Lir or Manawydan fab Llŷr is a Celtic Sea God, the Isle of Man is literally his island. Manannán is a Guardian of the Otherworld or Faerieland where there is no winter, no sickness and no falsehood. He is a powerful wizard who owned many magical items such as a cauldron of regeneration, a sword that would force people to tell the truth and a cloak of invisibility or sea fog that he used as a way to block access, when necessary, to his magical island or the Otherworld. Call upon Manannán for his guidance in your magical workings, especially if those workings involve working for the benefit of the waters of our planet or if you need helps speaking your truth.

Aquamarine and the Faeries of water also wish us to get more in tune with our own cycles and tides. Many people after all do find themselves very affected by the tides and the changing faces of the Moon, even if they don't live near the oceans. That's perfectly natural as we are made up of about 60 percent water and our hormones have tides, with the average female cycle being about the same as the cycle of the Moon. This also applies to our emotions, as Mermaids and other Faeries of water are very in touch with their true selves, their inner beauty and their emotions. It is this that gives them their power and they want us to fulfil our potential and find our own inner power too. Meditating with or wearing Aquamarine can help us to better tune into these natural tides within ourselves. As a stone linked with the Throat Chakra, with speaking truth and traditionally said to have been helpful for sore throats and public speaking, many people like to wear Aquamarine jewellery over or close to their throat.

Selkies in particular, such as the Gwragedd Annwn, want us to be true to ourselves. No matter how long Selkies stay on land with their seal skins or true natures hidden, in the end the Selkie or Gwragedd Annwn always returns to their true nature and to their watery home. This doesn't mean that we don't change and evolve in life, just that we need to be honest with ourselves about who we are, no matter what faces or facades we wear for others.

Aquamarine is linked to the power of the ocean tides and the force of the waterfall. It represents your emotions and intuition, your tears, fears and your subconscious. Its lesson is to go with the flow, to listen to your inner self, attune yourself to your emotions, use your natural intuition and natural psychic ability, and develop them if you can.

In Norse legends and lore the Fossegrim and some Nix, both of whom were lonely and music-loving Faeries who dwelt in waterfalls, seem – for the most part – to have been considered particularly friendly to humans; so much so that in 1281 an Icelandic bishop made a ruling that forbade Icelanders from 'waking up Trolls or Land-Wights in waterfalls...'[35]

Water, just like the Mermaid's magical mirror, is a reflective surface that can also be seen into. In many cultures Faerieland or the Otherworld can be accessed via waterways; this is probably the reason for all those beautiful ancient votive offerings along the Old Sweet Track in Somerset and at Llyn Cerrig Bach in Wales. With Aquamarine, and indeed all Beryl stones, we are encouraged to look beyond and to look within for wisdom, guidance and answers, be it staring into a pool of water, a scrying mirror – like the Evil Stepmother in the Fairy Tale of *Snow White* with her *'Mirror, Mirror, on the wall...'* or into a crystal ball. Interestingly many of the earliest crystal balls were in fact made of Beryl, like the famous ball of the Elizabethan wizard Dr John Dee, and even some of the first eyeglass lenses were also made of Beryl, which is why in German glasses are called *Brillen*, deriving from Beryl.

A wonderful way to cleanse your crystals and to connect with Aquamarine and the Faerie beings of water, is to wash your crystals in water from a local holy well or spring – even better if it is a local Fairy well! There are many such sites all over the world, although they may not be well known and can be exceedingly well hidden. It is well worth checking out your library's local studies section, as many county-specific or area-specific books have been written on local holy wells. Surfing the web can also be helpful as there are many holy well enthusiasts blogging about and recording such wells for posterity. In return for the Faeries' blessings on your working with water and crystals, and to generally say thank you, you might like to pick up rubbish from the site or your local beach or join an organised beach/holy well/river clean up – it can be a really rewarding experience that deepens your connections to these magical watery beings.

Aventurine

Other Names: Often misspelled as Adventurine. Green Quartz, the Gambler's Stone or the Lucky Stone

Chemical Composition: SIO_2 The green hues and the specks are from Fuchsite Mica inclusions $(K(Al,Cr)_2AlSi_3O_{10}(OH)_2)$

Element: Earth, woodlands and nature

Season: Spring

Planet: Venus, Earth

Chakra: Heart and Earth Star

Birthstone: August, Aries and Libra

Other: Day stone for Fridays

Faerie Monarchs/Deities: All those linked with fertility and abundance, e.g. Freyr/Ing, Freyja, Abundantia, Rosmerta, Isis and Rana Nieda

Faeries: Elves, Dryads, Flower Faeries, Anthousai, Plant Faeries, Devas, Leprechauns, Lieschi or Lesovikha and Gille Dubh

The name Aventurine derives from the Italian *a ventura* meaning 'by chance'. Like many other green stones, Aventurine is associated with abundance and was thought to attract wealth, plenty and good fortune. Because of this it has long been a favourite with gamblers, it is even sometimes known as 'The Gambler's Stone'. It has the luck of the Irish, the luck of the four-leaved clover and the luck of the Leprechaun to it, and is in fact beloved by the Leprechauns for its lucky energy as well as its green hue.

Aventurine ranges in colour from light to dark green with a kind of silver, Elven undertone to it, which identifies this as especially beloved by the Faeries of pretty much any and every kind. Green has long been considered a Faerie colour and you will find time and time again that Faeries are said to wear clothes of green. Its green colour promotes balance and harmony and it has a sense of freshness and revitalisation to it. This is also the green of the Green Ladies, who are Spirits or Sprites that serve as guardians of families and homes – no matter how small or how grand. The Green Lady of Skipness Castle in Scotland has watched over the castle and its associated families for generations, as has the Green Lady of Caerphilly Castle who can sometimes be seen among the ivy that grows upon its towers[36]. Many Mediaeval churches also have Green Lady or Green Man (see Moss Agate) guardians watching over them and their congregations. Ivy has a bit of a bad reputation for taking over, but it provides a very valuable safe haven for all sorts of birds and insects. Ivy grown in the garden, or even in a pot on a windowsill if you lack a garden or want to keep it under control, can really help cleanse an area of negative energies and harmful toxins[37]. Most importantly, it can provide a place for a Green Lady to live so that she can watch over you, your family and your home. Ivy can make a lovely addition to your Faerie altar to connect you with the natural world and help the Faeries feel right at home.

Aventurine teaches us of the way that everything in life is intertwined. It reminds us of the spiral growth pattern of nature, which links to the spiral movement and cycles of the planets and stars. It also shows us of our need to have a special refuge away from the bustle and pressures of modern life. Aventurine has a tenacious energy, teaching us about our own tenacity and our ability to thrive, even in difficult circumstances.

Aventurine helps connect us to the natural and Devic world. It is a stone beloved by gardeners and anyone who works with plants or herbs, as it helps plants and indeed humans to grow and thrive. Aventurine stones places around plants will help them be strong and healthy and help the Plant Faeries, the Flower Faeries and the Anthousai (Flower Nymphs) who live within your plants know that they are welcome and appreciated. It's the birthstone for those born in August and in Anglo-Saxon August was aptly known as *Weodmonath* or 'Weed Month', because weeds grow like crazy at that time of year[38]. Aventurine has long been used for healing and magical purposes when growth is needed, for example to help babies and children grow up healthy and strong, to convalesce after a long illness, to help manifest abundance and wealth, or to increase the effect of spells. It should never be used with anyone with a virus, cancer or with inflammation or anything else that you really do not want growing or thriving.

As a stone of fertility it is the gemstone of the Norse God or King Freyr, also called Ing. Freyr was known as the bringer of peace and harmony. He was often called on to bring favourable growing seasons and bountiful harvests[39]. Freyr may even be the original Tooth Fairy as he was given *Alfheim* – 'Elf Home' – which was the Norse World of the Elves, for his teething present[40]. As Ing, Freyr also gives his name to the Rune of fertility and potential. Ing is the potential, growth and green energy of the mighty oak within each little acorn and shows us our own potential, especially our own creative potential. From Ing we also get the word inglenook, that little nook by the fire in old houses. This inglenook was often the favourite spot of the household Brownie and we can use the Rune Ing, with its diamond shape, to create a safe space for the Faeries and Brownies to inhabit or to create a sacred and safe space for magical workings. If you don't have an inglenook in your home, create one to help your household Faerie or Brownie feel welcome.

Aventurine and its associated Faeries are also linked with the freshness and birth/rebirth of spring and purification. Faerie Queens and Goddesses such as Isis, Rana Nieda and Brighid were said to bring about the greening of spring. It is very much the stone associated with the fresh energies of the birch tree. Birch twigs have long been used in saunas and were used to make the brush part of besoms, which swept out the old, stagnant energies and brushed in the new positive ones. Aventurine can also be used to metaphysically do the very same thing. The silver birch was also thought to have been a portal to the Otherworld. Other names for the birch are 'Lady of the Woods' or 'Lady of the Greenwood', referring to the Dryads that live within them with whom we can commune with by working with the birch or with Aventurine. In Russian folklore the birch is home to the *Lieschi* ('male spirit of the forest') or *Lesovikha* ('female spirit of the forest') and Scottish legends tell us that the Gille Dubh is a Tree Guardian Faerie who is especially fond of birch trees. Many local Land-Wights and Faeries who live within or near Faerie Mounds also adore the birch[41]. All of these birch and Aventurine-loving Faeries often challenge us to do something new before they will work with us or ask us to approach them in the same was as we would if we were still innocent children full of wonder.

Aventurine is often incorrectly spelt as Adventurine, but this is very apt as this stone can motivate and inspire us on our adventures in life, encouraging us to take on new challenges and learn new skills, or just to look at things in a whole new way. A stone of the heart and Heart Chakra, it soothes anger and instead promotes compassion for all living beings as it helps us relate to others better on an emotional level. It can also help us to gain and nurture friendships, with humans, animals, Faeries, plants and crystals.

Aventurine, with its link to abundance, is the stone of Abundantia and Rosmerta, two Roman Faerie Queens who personified abundance, prosperity and plenty. They are often shown with a Horn of Plenty or Cornucopia filled with fruits, nuts and bread symbolising abundance and nourishment. We can work with Abundantia and Rosmerta to bring prosperity and abundance into our lives, and this doesn't just mean wealth in the monetary sense, but also wealth of knowledge, an abundance of good friends and an abundance of Faerie blessings.

Carnelian

Other Names: Canary Stone, Cornelian or Sard

Chemical Composition: SiO_2. Its red colour comes from the inclusion of one or more of the many types of Iron Oxide

Element: Fire

Season: Summer and autumn

Planet: Mars and Jupiter

Chakra: Sacral

Birthstone: July, August and Virgo.

Other: Day Stone for Thursdays, National Stone of Sweden and Norway

Faerie Monarchs/Deities: Thor and Vesta/Hestia, Nusku, Arinitti and Gabija

Faeries: Fire Sprites, Jagaubis, Hearth Sprites, Fire Sprites, Salamanders and Fruit Faeries, the Faeries and Dryads of the rowan and hawthorn

The name Carnelian, or Cornelian in its older form, comes from the Latin *Cornum*, referring to the cornel cherry or cornelian cherry dogwood, the reddy-orange fruit to which Carnelian bears a resemblance. Its other name of *Sard* comes from the Persian word *sered* meaning 'yellowish-red' alluding to the stone's colour. Carnelian can range from a very light orange to a deep cherry red. It has a much softer energy than many other red stones, probably because its red is less intense and it is often creamier in colour.

Carnelian has long been a very popular stone; there are some beautiful examples of Carnelian jewellery and ornaments from Mycenae, Ancient Egypt, Greece, Syria and Phoenicia. Mohammed, Napoleon I and Napoleon III were all said to have worn Carnelian. Carnelian was and still is a popular choice for signet or seal rings because wax doesn't stick to this gemstone.

Due to its link to the cornel cherry and the fact that traditional crystal lore its healing properties include regulating all bodily fluids, healing digestive issues and aiding vitamin absorption – especially from fruit – Carnelian is closely linked to all fruit and berry-bearing trees such as cherry trees, holly trees, apple trees and especially the rowan tree and hawthorn. It is also linked to all the Fruit Faeries who work hard bringing the fruits to ripeness. Placing Carnelian stones around your fruit-bearing trees and shrubs supports the Fruit Faeries in their work. Hawthorn bears a fruit the colour of Carnelian called a haw or Pixie pear, and it is the ultimate Queen of the Faerie trees. As Katharine Briggs says in *The Fairies in Tradition and Literature, 'Hawthorn trees…are everywhere thought of as haunted by the Fairies.'*[42] Faeries dance in rings around hawthorn trees as humans do around the maypole – which takes its name from the may tree. Here it is also worth noting that Carnelian and its Faeries are also connected to the poisonous and hallucinogenic Fairy mushroom amanita muscaria or fly agaric, which they also love to dance around, because the top of the mushroom is the colour of Carnelian.

Carnelian is undoubtedly the special stone of Thor – the Norse God of Thunder – and it can be found in Scandinavia, just like the legends of Thor himself. Thor has a reputation as a killer of Giants, but the truth is he can just as often be found socialising with Giants, such as his sometimes friend/sometime enemy Loki, as slaying them. Thor, like his father Odin and several other Gods, is also descended from Giants, which are of course a Faerie-type being. Thor is a very powerful and much beloved God of Fertility, Storms, Strength and Hallowing. Carnelian helps us to connect to Thor and to call on him to help us to find our courage and our strength.

Carnelian also has that fiery energy of Thor to it and, being associated with fire, it is also a stone loved by the Fire Sprites, the Jagaubis – Lithuanian Hearth Sprites, the Salamanders and the Roman Faerie Goddess of the Hearth, Vesta, and her Greek version Hestia, as well as countless other Hearth Deities and Sprites. We can work with Vesta/Hestia and these Fire Faeries through hearth fires, candles or even the flames of a modern gas hob as well as via Carnelian stones – which are probably the most mobile and practical of these options. Vesta/Hestia, Thor and their fiery friends can help us ignite our own inner fires for creativity (which the Celts called 'Fire in the Head'), to tend our inner Divine Spark, or to ignite our passions. In crystal healing, Carnelian is linked with fertility, the Sacral Chakra, the human reproductive system and our hormones. Carnelian is the fire of our very life force, the electrical sparks that keep our brain and hearts going and the fire that is our personal will and power. Holding or meditating with Carnelian can help motivate, revive, inspire us and can help us to find our get up and go, even if it feels as if it has got up and gone somewhere else. Traditionally Carnelian was worn or placed near pregnant women as they gave birth as it is said to help us with birthing, be it the birthing of a baby or the birthing of new ideas and projects. It can help improve the memory and concentration as it invigorates both mind and body.

It is popular with crystal workers, mystics, Tarot readers, Faerie card readers and diviners, who often keep a Carnelian with their crystals, cards or tools as the invigorating and cleansing energy of Carnelian and its associated Faeries helps keep their energies clear and clean. Carnelians placed around the home can have the same effect, helping to cleanse, rejuvenate and brighten the energies of your home. Carnelian stones can also help you to provide a home for Fire Sprites if for any reason a flame is impractical in your magical workings or domestic surroundings.

Cassiterite

Other Names: Tin Ore, Tin Spar or Tinstone/Tin Stone
Chemical Composition: SnO_2
Element: Metal
Season: All
Planet: Jupiter
Birthstone: Scorpio, October and November
Anniversary: The tenth wedding anniversary
Other: County Gemstone for Cornwall
Faerie Monarchs/Deities: Joan the Wad and Jack O' Lantern
Faeries: Pixies

The name *Cassiterite* derives from the Greek word for 'tin' – *kassiteros* because it was, and still is, the main ore that tin is extracted from. In the ancient Classical world, especially in Greece and Phoenicia, Britain was known as the *Cassiterides* – 'The Isles of Tin' – because of its plentiful supply of tin, especially in the southwest of Britain. Britain's vast mineral wealth was also one of the main reasons that the Romans twice decided to try to conquer these islands.

Cassiterite's importance as tin ore has meant that the beauty of Cassiterite has often been overlooked. They are exquisitely beautiful shiny crystals that range in colour from deep black, through brown and red to yellow.

The best known Otherworldly inhabitants of the southwest of Britain are the Pixies of Cornwall, Devon and parts of Somerset. There are various forms of the name including Piskie, Pigsie or Pizkey. However, be careful never to call a Pixie an actual Faerie as there is enmity between the two races – there has even been a battle between them at Buckland St Mary (the Pixies won, in case you were wondering). Pixies absolutely adore and are very closely associated with Cassiterite and tin in all its forms. Even today you can buy little Pixies cast from tin, pewter (an alloy predominantly made with tin) or from bronze (an alloy of tin and copper) to bring you luck and carrying a piece of Cassiterite will also bring you luck and put you on the Pixies' radar.

The King of the Pixies is Jack O' Lantern, best known to us these days from carved lit pumpkins and their Queen is Joan the Wad (*Wad* being a dialect word for 'Torch'). Both of these Monarchs are Will O' the Wisps whose mystical light might lead travellers astray or lead them home as this old rhyme shows:

Jack-the-lantern, Joan-the-wad,
That tickled the maid and made her mad,
Light me home, the weather's bad[43].

We can ask Jack and Joan to light our way in life, to lead us physically or metaphysically home if we feel that we have lost our way or direction in life.

Joan the Wad is also well known for bringing good luck to those who respect her. In the last couple of hundred years little figures of Joan have been carried or placed in the home to bring good fortune and there's a lovely collection of several such items in The Museum of Witchcraft and Magic at Boscastle in Cornwall. This is the origin of another old rhyme:

Good fortune will nod,
If you carry upon you Joan the Wad.[44]

Mostly Pixies are mischievous and benign to humans. They love dancing, wrestling and playing tricks on just about everyone and everything, although they can and do get overly carried away sometimes. Pixies are particularly fond of children and love to play with them. In physical appearance and temperament they are often described as 'childlike', no matter how wizened or ancient they are and this is because they keep in touch with their inner child who loves to simply have fun. Pixies are always urging us to have more fun and to be in touch with who we were as children when the world was still so magical, special and full of wonder. They encourage us to laugh, to celebrate life and to revel in joy.

By working with the energies of Cassiterite we can connect with the Pixies and their sense of cheekiness and fun. Cassiterite crystals have that deep twinkle to them that the mischievous have in their eyes. Cassiterite can be used to lighten the spirit and to help us let go of past hurts and traumas. Pixies know that we each have a thousand reasons why we have become more jaded and 'adult' as we have grown up. They respect that (somewhat grudgingly), but they want us to learn from life and to forgive and let go of all that has hurt or harmed us in any way so that it can no longer harm us or weigh us down, either figuratively or literally, for Cassiterite has been used traditionally to help with the management of weight issues and to find underlying causes for weight gain or loss. This is also true of harm done to us in past lives that we still may be carrying into this one as well as what we've lived through in this life. Through Cassiterite they want to help us heal our inner child and all that has been done to it to restore it to its true magical self that is able to have fun and enjoy life. They also really want us to help each other with healing our inner children so that their joy and vivacity can be shared with as many people as possible.

In Devon and Cornwall Pixies also serve as guardians and inhabitants of old stone circles, dolmens, barrows and cairns as well as many natural rock features and coves, and many such places or features are even named for the Pixies such as Piskey's Hall Fogou, Pixies' Parlour, Pixies Ring and Pixies Rocks. As with the resident Elves in Iceland, Pixies have no qualms about playing tricks on those who would damage, build on or frack under their ancient stone homes in order to protect them. So if you are called to speak out or protest against the desecration or damage of old sacred sites, do call on the Pixies and Elves for their assistance. Pixies and Elves can also help us to guard our own stone features and crystals, even your home if it made of stone, watching over them and guarding them. That said they will also help themselves and play with any stones so you can find a few going wandering sometimes! I've found that keeping a Cassiterite stone or a little tin Pixie with my crystals and rocks can give them a particular item to play with to their heart's content so that they tend to watch over the others rather than hide them.

Cassiterite has a very cheerful yet very deep energy. It knows that we are soulful beings with depth and takes us safely down within our depths and shadow self to safely work things through and emerge brighter, lighter and 'shinier', having embraced our true selves and let go of anything that was dragging us down. It is especially beneficial for helping us to work through anxiety issues and the stresses that we face as part of our modern lives. These crystals also underline our own mortality, not in a negative way, but rather in teaching us to celebrate life and to live it to the full each and every day.

Clear Quartz

Other Names: Cornish Diamond, Rock Crystal or Crystal Quartz

Chemical Composition: SiO_2

Element: Ice and Fire

Season: Winter and summer

Planet: The Sun, Neptune and Uranus

Chakra: All chakras, especially Third Eye, Crown and Soul Star

Birthstone: April

Other: Day Stone for Sundays and Mondays, State Mineral of Arkansas and State Gemstone of Georgia, National Stone of Belgium and Switzerland

Faerie Monarchs/Deities: All, especially Jack Frost

Faeries: All, especially the Land Wights or Faeries of Place all over the world, the Ice Faeries, the Elves and Faeries of the Far North and Mountain Faeries or Giants

Quartz is the second most abundant mineral in the Earth's continental crust and is found all over the world. It comes in many forms and many colours: Amethyst is purple Quartz, Rose Quartz is pink Quartz and Smoky Quartz is brown Quartz, for example. Quartz can also be found within many other minerals, such as granites. The name Quartz derives from a Saxon word for 'vein ore' or 'hard'. In many of the Scandinavian and Germanic languages Rock Quartz is called something akin to the German and Swedish *Bergkristall* meaning 'Mountain Crystal' because they are intrinsically linked with the mountains and the Wights, Etins or Giants who live on or in them.

Quartz has been popular throughout history and prehistory and has been revered by almost all ancient cultures. To the ancient Japanese, Quartz represented Chi or the solidified breath of the Dragons of Creation, in India it was thought to be able to detect poisons, and Australian Aborigines and Native Americans used it in rainmaking ceremonies. Quartz could also be found in Chinese temples and it was a constituent part in the stones used in Northern European stone circles.

The ancients thought that Clear Quartz was water that had been frozen so cold and hard deep within the Earth that it would never melt. The word 'crystal' is from the Greek *Krystallos* meaning 'ice cold'. It is for this reason that Clear Quartz, also called Rock Crystal, is associated with the two Ice Giants of our solar system – Neptune and Uranus and the Rune Is, which represents ice and is the form of an icicle. The Anglo-Saxon Rune Poem describes Is elegantly: *'Ice is very cold and immeasurably slippery; it glistens as clear as glass and most like to gems; it is a floor wrought by the frost, fair to look upon.'* Like Ice, Clear Quartz is certainly fair to look upon and it certainly does have a very cold feel to it. As ice is energy contained and still, with Clear Quartz there is also the sense of the energy contained within it, waiting optimistically for that energy to come forth or to find its purpose. Yet Clear Quartz also contains the energy of fire as it can focus the Sun's light to start a fire, which is why it is a good idea never to leave any clear form of Quartz in direct sunlight.

Clear Quartz has the clarity of pure ice and can help us to focus in and see things more clearly. If you are studying, researching or seeking wisdom in any way, Clear Quartz helps promote mental focus, memory, energy, and concentration. It can clear and clarify our mind, body and soul, helping us to find inner clarity and inner peace in a busy, bustling and chaotic world. Yet oddly enough Quartz and its Faeries have helped make this world what it is today. Our computers, telephones, credit cards, watches, TVs and many other technologies rely on Quartz to function. Quartz and its Faeries want us to be informed, to be able to communicate with each other across vast distances, just as we communicate with the Faeries across the veil. By communicating with our fellow humans from all over the world we are actively breaking down humanity's self-imposed barriers, which in turn breaks down dangerous 'us and them' thinking so that we can see ourselves for what we truly are – one large and amazing family of people whose differences are to be celebrated not denigrated. Quartz crystals take this even further and highlight the fact that all creatures, all sentient beings and all things – animals, plants, rocks, stars and Faerie beings – are all part of one great family, and that working together for the higher good and good of all is in all our interests. Importantly Clear Quartz facilitates communication between all beings and most noticeably with higher and spiritual beings. Quartz is believed to help us attune to the one great Universal Energy that is in all things, and is a popular stone with Reiki Masters as well as Faerie workers.

Time in Faerieland works differently to in our world: people who have visited Faerieland for what they thought was an evening turn out to have been away for a hundred years. As the Ice Faeries and Faeries and Sprites of Quartz also govern mortal time via our Quartz-driven clocks, we can ask them for help with our time management issues and to help us find more time in the day. They are especially agreeable to this if we are asking for help to find the time to create, to care for nature, ourselves and others.

Quartz shares ancient wisdom with us and forces us to see through the notion that our ancestors were stupid or uncivilised just because they lived different lifestyles to us. Quartz is said to hold all the wisdom in existence, past, present and future and it invites us to look within it to seek answers and unlock its mysteries. Clear Quartz is the crystal of creativity and the creation of all things as it embodies both ice and fire because in the Norse creation legend The World of Fire – Muspelheim or matter – collided with the World of Ice – Niflheim or anti-matter – and created the universe[45] and the Big Bang. Working with the Faeries of Ice, who bring crystalline beauty to a harsh cold world, and the Faeries of Fire, who create the heat that enlivens and warms our souls, inspires us to create, write, sing, paint and craft in a myriad ways, bringing beauty and pleasure to ourselves and those who see our work.

This is the best all-round healing stone because it contains a rainbow of all the other colours and energies. Clear Quartz can be used to refract light to make rainbows and to create our own Rainbow Bridge, like the Bifrost Rainbow Bridge in Norse legend, to connect our world, the world of man, to the other worlds and connect us to the Faeries in a positive, bright and magical way.

When you hear the word 'crystal' in old stories and fairy tales, the crystal in question is probably Clear or Snow Quartz. The great crystal castles of Gwynn ap Nudd and Arianrhod are probably of Quartz, as is the great crystalline Faerie castle in the Mediaeval tale *Lanzelot.*

Round or faceted Clear Quartz crystal balls have been found in many Pagan Anglo-Saxon and Viking burials. These balls are either held within a metal cage or simply have holes in from which they were strung and worn as necklaces or from girdles. What these crystal balls were used for is highly contested. Modern mystics believe that they were used as 'crystal balls' for scrying or gazing or communicating with the Otherworlds, while archaeologists prefer to believe that these were used to either make fire or as curing stones, where the stone is dipped into water to bless it or give it magical powers[46]. Later, in Christian times, Clear Quartz crystals and pebbles were associated with the purity of the Virgin Mary.

Crystals of Clear Quartz have the ability to magnify and amplify. They can be used as magnifying glasses to enlarge print, they can also help magnify and amplify any energies that we are working with, especially in our healing work. Conversely it can also magnify and reveal our flaws, but here we can ask the

Faeries, especially the Ice and Frost Faeries ruled over by Jack Frost, to turn our flaws into something positive and as beautiful as those fern-like ice designs that form on objects in the bitter cold. Just as the flaws make every stone of Clear Quartz unique, our flaws make us human and unique. Here we cannot hide our flaws from the light, but we can work with the light and the Ice Faeries to see and understand them clearly in order to learn from our flaws and to heal them. In this same way Clear Quartz can help us to clearly see into our own health and wellbeing as well as the situations we find ourselves in to see the real root causes of any issues, unease or dis-ease. Clear Quartz promotes the flow of healthy and positive energy and deflects negative energies like a shield of pure ice and light. Placed over the Chakras, Clear Quartz helps us to see the health of each Chakra and to clear any blockages or shadows from them. Though it can be used with all Chakras, it is most closely associated with the Crown, Third Eye and Soul Star Chakras as it helps show us our spiritual purpose and enhance our psychic abilities. Clear Quartz and the Faeries invite us to see our gifts and skills as a way to help others as well as ourselves and to seek help from others when necessary, because we all have within us a spark of the Divine and our own unique set of divinely given gifts and skills.

Should you find the energy of Clear Quartz a little overwhelming, Snow Quartz is a gentle alternative.

Elf Shot/Elf Arrows (Flint Arrowheads)

Other Names: Flint, Thunderstone, Chert, Firestone or Hornstone
Chemical Composition: SiO_2
Element: Deep Earth
Season: Winter
Planet: Earth
Chakra: Base
Birthstone: Birthstone for all humans regardless of when or where we were born
Other: State Gemstone of Ohio
Faerie Monarchs/Deities: Diana the Huntress, Fortuna, the Fates or Norns, Gaia/Terra, Hathor, Mother Earth
Faeries: Elves, Salamanders, Fire Sprites, Dísir, Gnomes and Land Wights

Stones and pebbles of flint are often considered quite boring nowadays, but they really are very special, powerful and important stones, whether in their natural form or shaped and utilised by mankind. Flint is a hard, sedimentary crystalline form of Quartz that forms as nodules within sedimentary rocks such as limestone or more commonly chalk. The outside of the nodule usually has a waxy, pale appearance, but once opened the inside of the nodule has a glassy appearance and can be black, brown, grey, beige, white, green or even on rare occasions blue. This huge difference between the exterior and interior of Flint nodules exemplifies all of us, for who and what we are on the inside is not always shown on our exterior. Many Faerie beings in Faerie tales may appear beautiful on the outside, but are in fact ugly on the inside while many ugly hags later reveal their real inner beauty to questing knights. Flint stresses the importance of our inner innate selves, our inner beauty and our inner magic.

Flint helped drive a revolution in ancient times; it was *the* stone of the Stone Age when mankind was making all sorts of practical and really rather beautiful tools from Flint and other stones. The name Flint derives from the Proto-Germanic *flintaz,* which itself derives from the even more ancient Proto-Indo-European *splind,* both words meaning 'to cleave or split'. Cleaving or knapping Flint was a valued skill and mankind opened the first mines, such as that of Grime's Graves in Norfolk, to extract Flint and the first factories to shape it. Flint tools were considered both mundane and magical and there's a lesson for us all there on how we live our lives, for we are magical beings living earthly lives, which is quite the challenge! Flint tools were considered a gift from the Earth or the Gods/Goddesses, they were then shaped and used for practical and religious purposes, and, once they were finished with, they were given back to the Gods/Goddesses in the form of votive offerings.

Flint and the Faeries and Elves who work with Flint are always trying to show us, usually pretty blatantly for these fellows are not subtle, that we need to use the right tool for the job or to be practical in the situation. For example, if we want to go back to college, praying and meditating over our decision is great to form and manifest the idea, but really to make it happen we are going to have to fill in that college application and get it sent it in. Here we are reminded that the power is within us and that we can make things happen by following through on our intentions with our actions. As with Flint knapping we are encouraged to chip or work away, little and often, to help manifest and make our dreams come true by bringing them down from the star plane where they exist as ideas down into the earthly plane where they can exist as truly real and tangible.

Flint can help the shy to boost their confidence. It motivates us into action and to end procrastination. It can also spark new ideas and new connections, like synapses firing within our brains. In this it has a very fiery energy and connects us to Fire Sprites and Salamanders, which is not surprising when you realise that Flint has been struck for millennia to make sparks to light fires, hence its byname of Firestone. It was also the Flint in the cock that gave Flintlock pistols their name and provided the spark to light the gunpowder. The fire of Flint is that of both life and vitality and of death. Fire warms and cooks our food, but fire can also burn and harm us, so as always we need to be careful and responsible for our actions and thoughts.

Flint as Firestone is linked with the Need Fire, represented by the Rune Nyd, which has the appearance of two sticks being rubbed together to make fire. This was the fire that cooked food and gave warmth long before the advent of central heating and ovens. This was also the fire that could transform ordinary looking stones into precious metals. This Rune and indeed Flint emphasise the difference between need and want, which differ considerably although they are often confused in this materialistic world in which we live. Here we are reminded of the magic and protection of the Faeries that are all around us, even in tough times.

Flint has been used decoratively in buildings, especially in East Anglia, for hundreds of years. Some classic examples are Burgh Castle, the stunning Holy Trinity Church at Blythburgh and Thetford Priory. Flint has been considered a protective talisman for thousands of years; its glassy side was faced outwards on buildings to deflect any bad vibes, ill wishes, curses, negative energies or negative entities away. Placing four pieces of Flint at the four corners of your home or property, with any glassy sides facing outwards is thought to protect the home from negativity while placing a piece under the bed is said to keep away nightmares – the original Night Mares were malevolent Goblins – and stop any Goblins or Boggarts from hiding under the bed. Flint stones are considered extra lucky and protective if they have a hole running through them – see Fairy Stone (Holed

Stone).

Neolithic arrow heads, also called *Elf-Shot* in England, Germany and Scandinavia, *Saighead Sith* – 'Sidhe/Faerie Arrows' in Ireland and Scotland, and *Pixie Shot* in Cornwall and Devon[47], were worn by Saxons, Vikings and Celts as amulets against Elf Sickness. Elf Sickness was any form of sharp, sudden pain of the kind that we'd think of as rheumatism, lumbago, a stitch or cramp. All of these ailments were all thought to be caused by being shot with Elven arrows[48]. Should someone be afflicted by these pains, these arrowheads would be placed or very, very softly rubbed over the problem to draw off the pain and discomfort. This is a truly ancient idea that probably goes back thousands of years. Our ancestors believed that the arrowheads were literally Elven arrows and so any passing Elves would think that the person carrying one had already been hit by one of their arrows and not waste any more arrows on them. If someone had already been hit the notion was that the wound could be undone by gentle use of another arrow. As these Neolithic arrow heads are sharp little weapons, we can also utilise Elf-shot to psychically cut away and cauterise any cords or attachments that no longer serve us for good or that are being used by others, accidentally or deliberately, to drain our energy. Elf-shot is very much an amulet of psychic protection and self-defence, but we must never use these to deliberately target or harm others as that removes their magic.

The ancient Flint arrowheads were made and used for subsistence hunting to support and provide for families, which is a world away from the pointlessness of game hunting for sport. Nowadays we understandably have a distaste for hunting animals, which is a very good thing, but we still go 'hunting' in other ways. We are all searching or hunting for meaning in our lives. We still provide for our families like our ancestors did, albeit through other means, and we go job hunting, house hunting and what is the favourite of many, bargain hunting!

That you are reading this book and interested in spiritual development also shows that you are on a quest like the knights of old, questing for knowledge, spiritual enlightenment or your own version of the Holy Grail. We work with these ancient arrowheads and call on Diana, a Faerie Queen and an ancient Goddess of Hunting, the Moon and the Wild to assist us in our modern hunting expeditions and to empower us on our quest for spiritual knowledge.

Because Flint is so ancient and has been used by mankind for so long, it can be used to help us to access ancient wisdom and the wisdom and guidance of our ancestors. Traditionally it has been utilised to access ancient memories and to assist in past life regressions. Here is it worth remembering that the Faerie races are ancient too and were sometimes considered or confused with ancestor spirits as with the Norse Dísir, who were both Faerie women and female ancestor spirits. It is also common for many Celtic families to have had at least one Faerie ancestor, for example the Welsh Pellings, and the Scottish MacLeods and MacPhees. It's also entirely possible that you are an incarnated Faerie being of some kind thereby having a spiritual Faerie heritage, if not a familial one. Working with Flint and the Faeries can help you discover your own deep and ancient Faerie connections.

Being such ancient stones and being linked with such ancient Faeries, Flints are connected with Fortuna – the Roman Goddess of Fate and Fortune, the ancient Fates or Norns who were Faerie women who controlled the destinies of Man. There were three Norns: *Urðr* –'Fate' who represented the past and was the eldest, *Verðandi* – 'Happening' who was the middle sister and represented the present and all that is happening in the here and now, and *Skuld* – 'Debt' or 'Future' who represented the future and was the youngest of the three. We can call on these three Norns to better understand our destinies and to guide us on our path in life and especially if we are performing a past, present, future Faerie reading or evaluating our life in any way. Fate was often considered to be a woven web, with our lives being a single thread within the web of threads that all touched and impacted on each other. Spinning features heavily in Faerie tales: Rumpelstiltskin spun straw into Gold and it was on a spindle that Sleeping Beauty pricked her finger on and from that she was destined or enchanted to sleep for a hundred years, but her destiny was changed by Prince Charming. The message of Flint is to understand that what we do in life affects the lives of others so we must always consider the needs of others as well as ourselves. Some have also used the glassy surface of Flint to scry or see into the future. Despite what some might chose to believe, our destinies are not set in stone and with the help of the Norns, the Fates or Fortuna, we can weave our own web of existence and change our destinies.

Flint's strong links to Mother Earth and the Mother Earth Goddesses like Gaia/Terra, Hathor and Mawu helps to keep us grounded and practical in our Faerie work and our lives in general, helping us not to get too 'airy-fairy' or too carried away by the Fae. We are after all in incarnate, earthly forms and tied to Mother Earth as well as being spiritual beings. A piece of Flint can ground you very effectively after any form of journeying, meditation or psychic work as it literally brings you back down to Earth. Flint can also help you to connect more deeply with our Earth Mother and the Faeries who live within her and tend to her, such as the Gnomes and Land Wights, and they have much to teach us about caring for and treading lightly upon our dear Mother Earth.

Elven Moonstone (Larvikite)

Other Names: Larvikite, Norwegian Moonstone, Black Moonstone, Norwegian Feldspar, Blue Pearl Granite or Monzonite
Element: Ice, Magic, Spirit and Cosmos
Season: Winter
Planet: The Moon
Chakra: Soul Star, Crown Chakra, Third Eye Chakra, Base Chakra and Earth Star
Birthstone: Birthstone of all us with a magical soul, especially for those born in the darker times of the year when the Northern Lights/Southern Lights can be seen more clearly, so October, November and December for those born in the Northern Hemisphere and for those born in May, June and July in the Southern Hemisphere
Other: Stone of Norway
Faerie Monarchs/Deities: The Faerie Guardians
Faeries: Elves, The Jotuns/Giants, Guardian Faeries, Maahiset/Maanväki, the Aurora Faeries, the Selkies and our personal Faerie Guardians

Usually grey with black inclusions, it may look quite boring at first glance, but do not be deceived for Elven Moonstone has a magical light hiding within it that it will show to those who quest to see the magic within the mundane. Elven Moonstone, as its name suggests, is a very magical stone closely linked with the Elves and other Faerie beings of Scandinavia, in particular those of Norway. It gets its common name of Larvikite from the Norwegian town of Larvik where it is mined. Highly prized for its schiller or labradorescence, Larvikite is used as a building material for facades and for fireplace surrounds. It is an igneous rock, having been formed by volcanoes and with its aurora-like shimmer, it definitely has a very fiery and very earthy energy to it.

Although its schiller is not as clear or brilliant as Labradorite, it can be quite amazing if you catch the light just right. As with Labradorite, its light comes in a range of colours all across the spectrum. It has a much darker, deeper energy that Labradorite or Moonstone, and it more closely linked with the darker half of the year and of the Moon's cycle. Its energy is like that of the aurora in the middle of winter. Working with Elven Moonstone during the long dark nights or when there is no Moon in the sky can be a very powerful experience. A perfect stone for night owls or those who thrive during the dark times of the year, it can also help summer and Sun lovers to learn to appreciate winter and darkness for their beauty and power.

Larvikite is the stone of the guardian. If you are the guardian of another person or their carer, especially another's child perhaps as an adoptive parent, foster parent or godparent, then this is a great stone for you. It is also ideal for all who act as guardian for a place or plot of land, whether it's your garden or if you're a park ranger/estate manager/woodland ranger, a curator of some kind or are a keyholder for your workplace. It is even suitable if you've simply felt moved to sign a petition to preserve or protect a woodland or sacred site, as it awakens our own guardian aspects and connects us to the Guardian Spirits of Nature. It encourages us to be protective of others – both people and places – and shows us how best to care for others in an empowering way.

Known by many names the world over, there are many Guardian Spirits of Nature. Some look after specific animals or trees while others care for specific places or areas. Common names for these Faeries include Land Wights, Rå (Swedish for 'Guardian') or Haltija (Finnish Guardians). These guardians often have specific roles. The Swedish Skogsrå ('Forest Guardian') watches over the forests while the Sjorå ('Sea Guardian') cares for the seas around Scandinavia. The Finnish Haltija also have very specific duties: the *Maan Haltija* ('Earth Guardian') protects the land, the *Kalman Väki* ('Death Folk') watch over graveyards and the dead, the *Kotihaltija* ('Home Guardian') protects the home and there are even Haltija who act as personal Faerie Guardians, a Faerie version of our Guardian Angels, who watch over and guide us. If you wish to connect to your personal Faerie Guardian try meditating with Larvikite or wearing a piece of Larvikite and allow them to introduce themselves to you in your dreams or visions. You may be lucky enough to see your personal Faerie Guardian like a flash of light just in the corner of your eye, just like the shimmer of this magical stone.

Larvikite is also the stone of the Scandinavian Earth-dwelling Faeries known as the Dark Elves, the Maahiset (Northern Saami), the Maanväki (Finnish) or the Underjordiska (Norwegian). These Faeries are guardians of the Earth and the land as indeed are many of the very misunderstood Jotuns or Giants of Norse legend. Thanks to pop culture we consider the Jotuns/Giants violent, monstrous and ugly, yet in the myths they could just as easily be elegant and beautiful like Skadi and Gerd, who was wooed by Frey. As with many other Faerie beings their appearance and mood depends on how they are treated, which is a healthy lesson for us all to be more pleasant to each other, then our very appearance will be more pleasant too! All of these Faeries are very powerful and possess potent magical powers. They encourage us to use our power to protect others and to protect places and Mother Earth. We're all familiar with the concept of the inner tiger/tigress coming forth to be protective of others and this is what these Faeries seek to help us to understand and emulate. The Faeries can help us to learn when to be protective and how best to be so, in order that we are able to make a real difference at the right time.

Larvikite is a very grounding stone, yet it can also raise our vibrations. It cleanses and heals our Auras and can heal gaps or problems within our Chakras, promoting a healthy, regular flow of energy throughout our energy system. Because it links both Base and Earth Chakras with the Crown and Soul Star Chakras, it can bring us visions, psychic dreams and enable us to use and develop or psychic and magical abilities in the everyday world as well as our more spiritual workings. Elven Moonstone shows us that, like the Elves, we too are magical beings with magical abilities and that magic is everywhere around and within us. If you are seeking magical knowledge or to enhance and develop your magical abilities and magical workings, Elven Moonstone is a wonderful and very instructive ally.

With its grey and black markings, Elven Moonstone is also the stone of the Selkies, the seal folk who live around the coasts of Norway, Iceland, the Faroe Islands and Scotland. In the water Selkies live as seals, but when they come onto land they shed their seal skins to take on human form. They show us the power of adaptability and transformation, of being or becoming something more. Like Mermaids, the Selkies teach us about our watery origins and how to go with the ebb and flow of life.

If you find yourself drawn to Norse legends and lore, the Norse Deities, have a deep love for Scandinavia and it's majestic landscapes, or have a liking for all things Viking, then you will adore the energy of Norwegian Moonstone. It can help you get in touch with any Scandinavian heritage that you may have, to connect to the Scandinavian Faeries and their monarchs or can assist you to understand the Norse myths on a deeper level.

With its calming energy, it can bring us a sense of spiritual calm, even in the hectic modern world, because it enables us to connect with the Earth below and the Heavens above. It is especially good for calming nerves and excess nervous energy, but conversely energises you if you feel sluggish. Elven Moonstone opens us up to the realm of the Faeries and the Elves, helping us to access their magic, wisdom and even to see and sense them around us. Keeping a piece near you will encourage the Faeries to watch over, protect and guard you and invoke their magical blessings. A very lucky stone, especially for those born in the darker part of the year.

Fairy Cross Stone (Staurolite)

Other Names: Staurolite or Croisette
Chemical Composition: $Fe_2Al_9Si_4O_{22}(OH)_2$
Element: Earth, Spirit and all in-between
Season: All year
Planet: All
Chakra: All
Birthstone: Pisces and December
Faerie Monarchs/Deities: All
Faeries: All

Staurolite Fairy Cross Stones form as black, brown or red twinned crystals in the shape of a cross. Although Staurolite can be found from Norway to Mexico, it is most famously found in Fairy Stone State Park in Virginia, USA, which is named after these magical stones due to a local legend. This states that when the local Faeries heard the sad news about Christ's death they wept and where their tears landed on the Earth they became these Fairy Crosses, which can still be found on and in the ground today[49]. In this the Faeries and the humans came together to mourn the death of Christ, sharing their grief.

Fairy Cross Stones are stones of compassion and of coming together to support each other through the good times and the bad.

Fairy Cross Stones connect us in a myriad of ways and show us that we are all connected to each other. We are all divinely created beings and connected through that Divine Spark within us all. We are all one great big family of beings and we are all connected through various lines of energy, friendships, associations and methods of communication. These lovely stones bring harmony to wherever they are placed, transmuting dissension and quarrels into peace in a way that means that everyone feels acknowledged and listened to. They can help us to find the middle ground in any situation for the very best of all involved, no matter how far apart peoples' opinions or ideas are. They can also help us to see things from another person's perspective so we can better understand why others think what they do and learn from that, expanding our own ideas and horizons.

Keeping a Fairy Cross Stone in the home is said to keep the household harmonious and ensure that everyone within the home is respectful of each other. It can help us to give each other space, the space to be ourselves and not feel frustrated or intimidated by others that we live or work with through either necessity of choice. Staurolite Fairy Crosses can help us cope with people who we might normally prefer to avoid for whatever reason, so are great to keep in your desk at work or in your pocket at work. They are ideal to have with you if you work with the public in any way to help you to better connect to your customers or clients in a friendly and positive way.

Fairy Cross Stones bring things or people together for a common cause or purpose. They are friendship stones, helping us to cement and strengthen existing friendships and to forge new ones. They can also help us to attract awareness and support for our ventures and even attract customers.

It is kindness, compassion, co-operation and tolerance that connects us all and keeps us all harmonious, and it is these same qualities that help us to connect to the Faeries and indeed to all living creatures and beings. We can achieve so much more when we work with like-minded others that we could ever do on our own, although our own individual contributions are of course incredibly valuable and important. Fairy Cross Stones inspire us to be patient and understanding with others, just as we would hope others would be the same with us. They help us to keep a balanced temperament so can dissolve away anger and anxiety, instilling us with a sense of calm and promoting good feelings towards others. We can learn so much from each other and have so much to learn from the Faeries. Working with the Faeries is a two-way process; we even have things that we can help them with and teach them!

While the Faeries love their excesses, and they really do, through Staurolite they highlight our need for everything in moderation. We cannot party like the Faeries or we lose something of ourselves or lose our time on this planet. They can get away with it because they live longer than us and in another realm, but we sadly have a more limited time and are grounded to a physical body. Staurolite is a great stone for those who naturally tend towards excesses, such as workaholics and those who struggle with addictions of any kind, as it helps us to moderate our excesses and understand the real issues behind them. When working through our issues, which run very deep indeed, the Faeries caution us for our need for patience with ourselves and others and remind us to be kind to ourselves. If you need support to help you through your issues, Staurolite can bring you together with support groups and people who can help you or who have successfully gone through the process themselves.

As Fairy Cross Stones bring things together, they can help us to find our true soul's purpose in life, bringing us tips and hints on what it just might be. All our projects and endeavours can start to come together with the help of the Faeries and their magical Fairy Cross Stones, if we are open to a bit of guidance from them, but these stones can also show us new directions to follow too so that we keep going and don't stagnate creatively or spiritually.

Traditionally Fairy Crosses have been used in magical workings to bring energies together harmoniously or to connect the magical worker with the magic of the elements or Faeries to enhance their work. It facilitates communication and the exchange of energies between our world and the magical Otherworld and ensures that we are working together for the higher good or a common cause and that we are doing so with love in our hearts and light in our souls. Fairy Cross Stones placed on a Faerie altar attract friendly Faeries into our lives who are naturally more aligned energetically with our own selves, meaning that we can quickly get a healthy and harmonious friendship going.

If you ever feel overwhelmed or overwrought by living on this planet with more than seven billion human souls and countless billion other living souls, then take a moment to meditate with a Fairy Cross Stone to find your own special and unique place in this world. You – like every one of those other souls – belong and are welcome here and loved for who you are and what you bring to this world.

When meditated with, these wonderful stones centre us beautifully in the here and now and can bring us a sense of inner peace. Even in our everyday lives Fairy Cross Stones bring a peaceful equilibrium to our existence. They can help us balance the needs of our head and our heart, and to juggle all the roles that we play in life, assisting us in finding a healthy work/life balance so we can find the time to live as spiritual beings on this earthly realm. Fairy Cross Stones are considered to bring good luck, protect their owner from black magic and disaster, and bring Faerie blessings, if properly looked after.

Fairy Crosses (Chiastolite)

Other Names: Chiastolite, Crucite, Chyastolith or Cross Stone
Chemical Composition: Al_2SiO_5
Element: Spirit, Earth and all in-between
Season: All
Planet: Earth
Chakra: All the human Chakras and all the Chakras of the planet Earth
Birthstone: Libra.
Other: State Mineral of Georgia
Faerie Monarchs/Deities: All, most noticeably Elen of the Ways, Ankou and Hecate
Faeries: All

Chiastolite is a form of Andalusite with a dark graphite cross feature that is revealed when the stone is cut. Technically the graphite cross is an impurity, but Chiastolite demonstrates how impurities, like our mistakes and detours in life, can be educational, beautiful and deeply meaningful.

Fairy Crosses also depict the Ley Lines, Energy Lines and Fairy Paths that crisscross our planet in all directions and depict the places of power where these lines cross. Ley Lines are a network of lines across the landscape discovered by archaeologist Alfred Watkins who wrote about them in his books *Early British Trackways, Moats, Mounds, Camps and Sites* and *The Old Straight Track: Its Mounds, Beacons, Moats, Sites and Mark Stones*. Watkin's Ley Lines are practical straight pathways or lines of sight, essentially the roads of their day, between ancient monuments such as stone circles, menhirs, henges and cairns and other natural features like hill tops and fords where people could safely cross rivers.

Energy Lines are the lines across the landscape through which energy flows; these are curving, sinuous and serpent-like and are often associated with Dragons or Dragon legends. Sometimes they literally are paths of Dragons such as the between Cadbury Castle and Dolbury Hill where Dragons were said to regularly fly between the two points. Energy Lines are akin to our own Energy Lines, or Meridians as they are sometimes known, which connect our Chakras up and down our body. The most famous of these Energy Lines in the UK are the St Michael and St Mary Lines, which crisscross their way from St Michael's Mount in Cornwall to Hopton in Norfolk and are wonderfully described by Paul Broadhurst and Hamish Miller in their book *The Sun and the Serpent*.

Fairy Paths, like Watkin's Ley Lines, are straight connecting lines between special Faerie sites, such as Faerie Rings, Elven Forests, Faerie occupied holy wells, Fairy Forts/Raths and other sites that are inhabited or frequented by the Fae. Some Fairy Paths are the same as known Ley Lines, some are not. Fairy Paths not only exist on land, they can go under water, act as causeways and go up very steep mountains. These Processional Fairy Paths are used by all Faeries, from those who live alone through to the masses of trooping Faeries, and even the Wild Hunt follows them. Some say the Wild Hunt is made up of the souls of the dead and others say it is Faeries riding out, either way these Otherworldly hunts are usually said to be led by Faerie Monarchs/Deities such as Frau Holle, Odin, Ankou or Gwynn ap Nudd.

Throughout the ages the blocking of Fairy Paths, or even just allowing cows to graze on them, has been said to bring misfortune. Many people are said to have been stolen away after happening upon or interfering with a Fairy procession along a Fairy Path. There are many tales, especially from Ireland, of families who have lost their luck or become ill after building on or across Fairy paths. The ways to undo this misfortune were:

1. To knock down the building completely
2. To alter the building so it no longer proved an obstacle
3. To leave a door or window at the front and back a little open overnight to allow the Faeries to continue on their path[50]

Nowadays you could put a Fairy Door in at the places where the Fairy Path crosses your property and that would allow them access.

In almost all cases where any of these steps were taken to allow free access again the fortune and health of the family were immediately restored. Here the message is crystal clear, Fairy Paths, like our own Meridians and Energy Channels, need to be kept clean and clear at all times. Here Chiastolite teaches us to take care of our own Meridians or Energy Lines to keep ourselves happy and healthy. It also encourages us to keep all of our connecting lines nice and healthy, so we're also talking about taking care of the lines that link us to others, such as friendship, and the lines that connect us to the Divine, such as our spiritual practices.

An old way to check if your property or any planned building was obstructing a Fairy Path was to place a pile of stones in what was or would be the corners of the building and to leave them overnight. If the stones were disturbed then it was a sure sign that the Faeries had moved them because they were in their way. Some Fairy Paths are clearly visible, as with Fairy Rings they can show up as darker lines in grass or lines where vegetation grows more vigorously.

The best known Fairy Paths are those at Penwortham in Lancashire, Mariner's Way on Dartmoor, *Sarn Bedrig* ('Road of St Patrick') in Gwynedd, the several *Sarn Elen* ('Road of Elen') in Wales, and the Rath Ringlestown Fairy Path near Tara in County Meath. You might also like to discover the Fairy Paths, Energy Lines and Ley Lines near your home, but be respectful and do not traverse them during the Faeries' special or sacred times such as dusk, dawn, under the Full Moon, or during the Old Fire Festivals, the Quarter Days or on Fridays – the Faerie holy day.

Fairy Paths are ruled over by two specific Faerie Monarchs: Elen of the Ways and Ankou. Ankou is the Breton personification of death and is also found in Welsh Legend as *yr Angau* and in Cornish Tales as *an Ankow*. He is the archetypical cloak-wearing skeleton, a scythe-wielding figure of death. Ankou is a Faerie King of Death who leads his subjects or the Spirits of the Dead along Faith Paths, or Spirit Roads as they were sometimes known, in order to get from this world to the Otherworld or the Next World[51]. Here we must recall that there is a great deal of confusion historically between Sprites and Faeries and the Spirits of the Dead. Ankou often called on those who were due to die to forewarn them of their fate. In this he was not cruel or evil, just giving the person a chance to put their affairs in order. Nowadays we see death and its personification as something devilish or to be scared of, but really Ankou is more like the character of Death in Terry Pratchett's Discworld novels in that he has a very important job to do, for it is Ankou's duty to safely herd up the souls of those who have died and see that they safely get to the Other Side. Chiastolite is also all about helping us with changes and transitions in life, such as changing jobs, moving house, transitioning from child to adult and even for transitioning from this life to the next.

The other Faerie Monarch who watches over Fairy Paths, and Chiastolite because it embodies these and other lines across the land, is Elen of the Ways. Elen is many things rolled into one and therefore a great role model for us all today. She is probably a half lost Celtic Goddess and Faerie Queen, although thanks to the Welsh Tales of the Mabinogion, she is now best known as Saint Helen of Caernarfon, wife of Maxim the Great and the mother of Constantine. She is often confused with another Helen, Helen of Constantinople, who also had a son called Constantine who was the famous Roman Emperor. In *The Dream of Maxen Wledig*, it is clear that Elen is Fae or touched by the Fae for she appears to Maxen in a dream and is described as wearing a white vest and being adorned and surrounded by red Gold[52]. Red and Gold are old Faerie colours. The tales tell that Elen ordered the making of a great Roman Road from Caernarfon to South Wales, which still bears her name today as *Sarn Elen* or 'Road of Elen' as do many other smaller roads in Wales, but the truth is that these roads predate the Roman era. Elen as Saint Helen of Caernarfon is a patroness of travellers and it would be lovely to think that she still watches over all the paths and roads of Britain, including the magical Faerie paths, ensuring safe passage for us all, humans and Faeries.

Chiastolite Fairy Crosses also teach us about the veil between this world and the world of the Faeries and how we can learn to literally cross over from our world to theirs and safely back again. We can work with Fairy Paths and Chiastolite to access the world and wisdom of the Fae as long as we are respectful and ask politely first. We can call upon Elen as protector and patron of all Britain's roads and paths to grant us safe passage and safe journeying in all forms. Fairy crosses have long been carried or worn as protective talismans on journeys, especially for any kind of spiritual journeying. Chiastolite Fairy Crosses, like those of Staurolite, act as shields to keep away those Faeries that might not be too agreeable to humans yet act as lanterns to show the more human friendly Faeries that we wish to engage with them and attract them into our lives.

The Fairy Cross of Chiastolite represents a crossroads and any such 'in-between' places are very popular with Faeries[53]. It is at a crossroads that Cherry of Zennor encountered the Faerie Gentleman[54] and Thomas the Rhymer journeyed to a cross roads with the Queen of Elphame that had three roads, one to Heaven, one to Hell and one between the other two that led to Faerieland. Chiastolite's cross also depicts the crossroads between the four magical Fairy Cities of Ireland (see Marbles of Ireland). Crossroads, including those held within Chiastolite, are traditionally presided over by the Witch Goddess and Faerie Queen, Hecate, who can assist with any and all kinds of transitioning or traversing. We all have our own paths in life, which all have their own ups and downs. We also follow different paths in the terms of spiritual belief, for there are many different faiths, religions and denominations in the world. The Faeries have their paths as we have ours and the secret is to always respect the paths and journeys of others. Sometimes our paths cross, sometimes they are side by side for long stretches, sometimes they diverge, but each of us can only walk our own path.

Chiastolite highlights the fact that our lives do not follow linear paths; we may find ourselves taking a very roundabout or winding path in life. We can even change some of the paths we walk, like our career path for example. Sometimes we find ourselves going two steps forward and one step back or completely backtracking in order to find another fork in the road. We can find ourselves at crossroads or even lose our way completely; though in truth the path is probably still there it is just that we need help to see it and here the Faeries can help us. Chiastolite shows us the path of our life: where we have been, where we are (which is the here and now as shown by the 'X *marks the spot'* of Chiastolite), and where we are going. The key to understanding Chiastolite, and indeed the Fairy Path, is that progression is the only way; we cannot stay still, we must always move on and move forward, whether mentally, emotionally, spiritually or physically. We may know where we are going, or hope to go, and have it all mapped out, or we may not have a clue and are just seeing where the road goes. Either way the Faeries with their wondrous and glamorous processions stress to us the importance of enjoying the journey for its own sake and to occasionally stop to smell the roses. After all, life is not a race.

Whatever path ahead we take, even if we are just meandering along, the Faeries will continue to support us as long as we continue to honour them and to make space for them in our lives.

Fairy Gold (Iron Pyrite)

Other Names: Fool's Gold, Iron Pyrite(s) or Brazzle/Brassle
Chemical Composition: FeS_2
Element: Fire, Earth and Metal
Season: Summer and autumn
Planet: Sun
Chakra: Solar Plexus
Birthstone: Leo
Faerie Monarchs/Deities: Oberon/Alberich and Elegast
Faeries: Dwarves, Leprechauns and Spriggans

Although it is best known as Fool's Gold due to the reputation for fraud and dishonesty that surrounds it because of the way it has been used by people to deceive others, Fairy Gold is actually a very beautiful and special mineral with an important message for us all. It is an Iron Sulphide with a brassy golden lustre that does resemble Gold and forms in vaguely cuboid shapes. The name Pyrite derives from the Greek πυρίτης (*pyritēs*), 'of fire' referring to the fact that Iron Pyrite, when struck, produces sparks that were used to light fires. Iron Pyrites were used in wheel lock weapons to 'fire' them. Pieces of Iron Pyrite have often been found as grave goods; in a practical sense they were probably deemed pretty useful for the deceased to take with them on their journey into the next life, but they may have also served a ritual or religious purpose[55].

In times past Fool's Gold was used to salt mines, to make people think there was Gold in them so they would buy into all sorts of dodgy scams, or sold to the unwary as Gold by the unscrupulous. Yet ironically – pardon the pun – Iron Pyrite is often found near Gold and Iron Pyrite even contains tiny traces of Gold! While Iron Pyrite may not be perceived to be as 'valuable' as Gold by many, its real magic and power is that it is just as valuable and has just as much to teach us as any other mineral. The Faeries know this and are only too happy to share this important message with those of us who are prepared to listen. Only the real fool cannot see what wisdom and practical purposes Iron Pyrite really has. Iron Pyrite is invaluable today for its use in batteries and solar panels, and as Iron Pyrite can start a fire, that can be of far more value to someone who is cold that a lump of Gold ever could be!

Though it may be the Gold of fools, Iron Pyrite been used in jewellery making since the time of the Ancient Greeks. Marcasite jewellery is not made from Marcasite at all, but from Iron Pyrite. After the death of Queen Victoria's husband, Prince Albert, mourning black and mourning jewellery were all the fashion so Marcasite was the perfect accompaniment for those who still wanted some bling, but in a very understated and sombre style. Victorian Marcasite jewellery is still sought-after today.

Many types of Faerie are renowned for their love of Gold. However, greed for Gold, or indeed anything, is not healthy, not for humans and not for Faerie Beings either. Frequently Gold hoards have been cursed by their owners so that if anyone else should possess it they will know nothing but sorrow. From Norse mythology comes the tale of Andvari's Gold: *Andvari* 'The Careful One', an allusion to his miserly nature, was a Dwarf with a magical golden ring, Andvaranaut, which could find or produce Gold. He lived under a waterfall growing rich until he was forced by Loki to give up both the ring and his hoard. In revenge Andvari forever cursed the Gold and whoever possessed it. Later on Andvari's Gold ended up in the hands of another Dwarf, or possibly human, called Fafnir. It affected Fafnir so deeply and so monstrously that he lost his human form and instead becomes the greedy 'green-eyed monster' that he was on the inside[56]. There's an important lesson here for humanity about materialism.

As we all know the Leprechaun hides his crock of Gold at the end of the rainbow or under a bush. Should a human ever manage to catch a Leprechaun, by some unwritten law the Leprechaun must reveal the location of his treasure. However, the Leprechaun is a cunning chap and will use a whole host of tricks to try and keep the treasure for himself[57], including providing the human with Fairy Gold instead of real Gold or by casting golden Faerie glamour onto something less valuable, such as fallen leaves. That said there are stories of when Leprechauns and other Faeries have chosen to share their wealth in whatever form with humans as an act of kindness or in reciprocation for an act of kindness from a human. Here the Faeries teach us about discernment and compassion. The ugly and unpleasant Spriggans of Cornwall also guard treasure, usually the kind buried in old barrows and ruins, and steal anything shiny to add to their hoard, including Fairy Gold, which is pretty ironic as most Faeries, including Spriggans, are thought to despise anything to do with iron.

Iron Pyrite is ruled over by two Faerie Kings: Alberich and Elegast. *Alberich* – 'Elf Ruler' is known to us from German mythology and Wagner's *Ring Cycle* operas and it is upon Alberich that Shakespeare based his character Oberon in *A Midsummer Night's Dream*. Alberich is a smith, a sorcerer, the King of the Nibelungen Dwarves and guardian of the Nibelungan treasure until it was stolen from him by Siegfried. Alberich explains to us that wealth is a means to an end, no more and no less. Wealth is a way to function and get by in a world that runs on money. Alberich shows us that material wealth is fleeting but that other types of wealth such as wealth of knowledge are the real treasures. Elegast whose name means 'Elf Spirit' is the Elven hero in the Mediaeval Dutch epic poem *Karel ende Elegast*. He may or may not be the same character as Alberich. Elegast is an Elven magician and thief, he can lull his marks into magical sleep and open locks without keys. In many ways Elegast is a Robin Hood type figure, robbing from the rich and giving to the poor so he can teach us a great deal about the flow of abundance.

Wealth, no matter what kind, is not meant to be hoarded, but shared so that as many people as possible can benefit from it.

Fairy Gold represents moveable wealth, spiritual wealth, the wealth of wisdom, the wealth of experience, abundance, achievement and nourishment. It teaches us to be charitable to others, not just in financial terms, but also to be compassionate. It also coaches us in discernment when it comes to matters of wealth. All too easily those who chase wealth can be deceived or fooled by appearances. What might look like a great get-rich-quick scheme is often a scam to separate us from our money rather than to make us money. Greed makes us easy to manipulate. Our gut feelings often know better and try to ward us off such scams, hence this mineral's association with our Solar Plexus Chakra, which is where we get those gut feelings. We reap what we sow in life, getting back what we put in. There are no quick fixes or easy get-rich schemes. Work and effort are what reaps rewards. Iron Pyrite and its Faeries encourage honesty in transactions of any kind, of honouring deals made and oaths given and warns against deceit or deceiving others.

If you are struggling with money worries or worry in some way that you do not deserve abundance, then Fairy Gold can enables you to work through outdated fears, concepts and ways of thinking about wealth, in particular material wealth. In past lives we may have suffered incredible poverty or taken a vow of poverty and that can impact on our relationship with abundance. Iron Pyrite and its many associated Faeries assist us in letting go of such negative baggage and to step joyfully into the flow of abundance and love that flows through all things.

Wealth and bounty in all their forms are gifts to us, from the universe, from Mother Earth, from the Divine. For us to truly appreciate them we need to comprehend their wealth and their value to us. The food that we eat, the Sun that lights our sky, the friendships that we have forged (just as precious metals are forged from dross), these are all valuable gifts that provide us with a wealth of joy. The Faeries wish us to share our abundance and to share our joy, not to hoard it like a miser. They inspire us to appreciate what we have. The Faeries are very aware that 'ownership' is a very strange human concept. We foolishly think we own things or own our own homes or land, but in truth we are short-lived caretakers of this planet with responsibilities to take care of it for future generations.

Wishful thinking, desires and flights of fancy can be no bad thing, but they can become obsessions that take over our lives and that's where things go wrong. There is a difference between fantasy and reality, which Pyrite's reflective sheen shows us in the same way as a magic mirror. Iron Pyrite encourages us to have our hopes and dreams and to place ourselves into the great flow of abundance that is there for all of us, but also ensures that we are not motivated by selfishness or greed. Iron Pyrite shows us that, like beauty, wealth is in the eye of the beholder, and shows every one of us how rich and blessed we are. Rewards and abundance do not have to be monetary, our achievements and the experience and wisdom that we have gained are our own crock of Gold! If we have our health, a roof over our head, someone who loves us, experience, knowledge, a job that we enjoy, children or pets who make us happy, etc., then truly we are rich.

Fairy Stone (Holed Stone)

Other Names: Hag Stone, Witch's Stone, Witch's Amulet, Hex Stone, Odin Stone, *Gloine nan Druidh* ('Druids' Glass' in Scots Gaelic), Maen Magi ('Stone of the Magi' in Welsh), *Glain Neidr* ('Adder Stone' in Welsh), Holey or Holy Stone

Element: Deep Earth, Water and Air

Season: Winter and those magical in-between days such as the Celtic Fire Festivals: Imbolc, Beltane, Lughnasadh and Samhain and the Four Quarter Days: Winter and Summer Solstices and Spring and Summer Equinoxes

Planet: Pluto

Chakra: Earth Star and Third Eye

Birthstone: Birthstone for all Faerie Workers, no matter when they were born

Faerie Monarchs/Deities: The Cailleach, The Elder Mother and Odin

Faeries: All, especially the Elves, Sylphs, Kurinyi Bog and the Kikimora

These stones have many names and are of many different materials, what they have in common is that they have a naturally formed hole running through them. These holes must be natural, usually caused by the action of water, and not made by man in order to be magical. It was often believed in times past that it was snakes, in particular adders, who created either the stone in its entirety from their saliva or secretions, or that the adder formed the hole in the stone by crawling through it.

These Holey Stones are often found on British, Dutch and German beaches and are considered extremely lucky tokens that bring their finder a bounty of good fortune[58]. According to tradition, for them to retain their luck they must be found or gifted, exchanging money for them removes their power.

These Fairy Stones are credited with many magical properties; they have been said to protect against bad Faeries, make people invisible, ward off the evil eye or any evil enchantment, cure snakebite, prevent nightmares and even heal whooping cough. They are considered most magical if they are hung up in or around a house or outbuilding with red thread – such thread is often used to deter evil witches and bad Faeries. Hanging Holey Stones in your home or by your Faerie altar is a sure way to attract good Faeries and let them know they are welcome in your life. Smaller Holey Stones can also be worn around the neck, attached to key rings or carried as Faerie-friendly talismans.

You may already have been lucky enough to have been gifted with a Fairy Stone, If not, allow yourself to be guided to find a very special Fairy Stone of your own. They are a gift and a sign from your magical companions that you are ready to begin working with them on a whole new level.

Looking through the hole, or holes, in the stone apparently allows us to see into the future, to see into the world of the Fae or Otherworld or to see Faeries[59], especially if we look through the stone at dusk, dawn, Samhain (October 31st), Beltane (May 1st) or any other in-between time. Holey Stones can be used in meditation, journeying and visualisations to access Faerieland if we 'see' ourselves travelling through the tunnel within the stone and through to the magical land of the Fae and back again. By looking through the hole we are also able to see beyond or through Faerie glamour or any facade or falsities to clearly see the absolute truth and the reality of a person or situation. They help us to see the truth and the Divine Truth in ourselves and in others. It is a lovely idea to keep a Holey Stone close by when you perform any kind of divination, especially using Faerie cards or Tarot cards, in order to clearly divine and 'see' the messages coming through and to provide psychic protection.

These holed stones have been popular for centuries, most noticeably with clairvoyants, psychics, witches and those who follow the Faerie Path, and are still very popular today with Faerie seers who use the stones to reveal or 'see' the mysteries of the Fae. They are the stone of the Faerie Sight or Second Sight – the ability to see Faeries[60], visions, Spirit, the future and other things to that are not present to the senses.

Many Faerie Monarchs are associated with the gift of wisdom, knowledge and prophecy. Sometimes these Holey Stones are called Odin Stones. Odin was a Norse God who famously gave up one of his eyes in exchange for a drink from Mimir's magical well of wisdom. Here we are warned about being careful what we seek or ask for. We are also reminded that sometimes we must make sacrifices in order to achieve or obtain something. Odin was a seer as his name attests: it derives from the proto-Germanic *Wōðanaz meaning 'Seer' or 'Prophet'. The term for the class of Druids known as seers, the 'Vates', also derives from a similar source. Odin is one of the figures that fed into the creation of Santa Claus. Like Santa, Odin was also acquainted with Elves. The word Elf comes from the Germanic Alf and the Svartalfs (Dwarves) created gifts for the Gods such as Odin's spear and a special ring that could magically duplicate itself. In the Runes Odin is represented by Os, which refers both to Odin the God and to a mouth. This is a mouth in terms of a human mouth from which breath and inspiration flows in and out and the mouth of an estuary from which water flows in and out. Odin was said to have given man the breath of life or his soul[61] and wisdom. Many of Odin's wise sayings have been recorded as the *Hávamál* – 'The Sayings of the High One/Odin'. According to Norse legend, Odin helped create the world around us from the corpse of the giant Ymir. His bones were used to make the mountains and his teeth were used to make rocks and boulders. Odin, Os and Odin Stones all speak to us of the great and ancient wisdom of the Earth, of the Deities and of the Faerie races. As the Anglo-Saxon Rune Poem tells us, '*The mouth is the origin of every speech, The support of wisdom and comfort of councillors, and* *to every man blessing and confidence.'* Odin Stones can help us to understand the language and energy of the Faeries and to join with and exist within the stream of great wisdom that flows in all directions.

As Hag Stones, these magical stones are closely connected to those wise, ancient Faerie Queen and Goddesses who were later demonised as evil old Hags. One such Crone Goddess is the Gaelic Faerie Queen and Goddess of Winter called The Cailleach or Beira. Her name means 'Hag' or 'Old Woman' today, but it also refers to her as 'veiled'. The Cailleach is truly the Queen of Faeries linked with the stones, rocks and minerals of the Earth, for she is credited with creating the mountains and hills in her wake. The stories tell us that The Cailleach deliberately created the mountains as stepping stones, while many of the boulders and rocks were created by accident when they fell from her basket or apron[62]. On Anglesey there is a passage grave known as *Barclodiad y Gawres* – 'Apronful of the Giantess'. In Glen Cailleach in Scotland, even today there is an old ritual involving stones and The Cailleach. Within the glen is a small farmer's hut, known as *Tigh nan Cailleach* – 'The House of the Cailleach' or *Tigh nam Bodach* – 'House of the Bodach (The Cailleach's Husband)' which house several large carved stones that represent the Cailleach, Bodach and their children. Every year these stones are placed outside, looking over the glen at the time of Beltane to bless the glen with fertility and are placed back in the shelter of the hut at Samhain[63]. You can do something similar at home if you like, to ask The Cailleach to bless your garden during the summer months. Find a stone that really speaks to you and seems to carry the wise, ancient energy of The Cailleach and place it outside, watching over your garden from Beltane to Samhain and place the stone somewhere sheltered such as a lovely tidy and clean spot inside your greenhouse or shed for the winter. By doing this you will also help attune yourself to the cycles and energies of nature, and therefore of the Faeries too.

Another Crone Faerie Queen linked with these holed stones is the Elder Mother who is found in tales from Britain, Germany and Scandinavia. The Elder Mother is the Spirit or Dryad of the elder tree who guards the door to the World of the Other, the Faeries or the Dead. She is associated with the darker mysteries and magic that exists and especially with the cycles of life, death and rebirth. It is considered very unlucky to fell an elder tree unless one asks permission first by making a specific promise: *'Old girl, give me some of thy wood and I will give thee some of mine when I grow into a tree.'* This is not meant as macabre or sinister, rather it refers to our body after death giving back to the soil and plants that helped provide for us in life. What goes around, comes around. Elder is one of the Faerie trees; in Scotland it was said that if you stood under an elder on Samhain then you would see the Elven Monarchs and their hosts of Elves, and in Denmark there was a similar version except that it had to be on Midsummer's Eve that you stood beneath the elder[64]. Wearing a crown of elder on May Eve is supposed to allow you to commune with the Otherworld and see Faeries and the Dead[65]. Faeries have also been said to make pipes from twigs and branches of the elder by removing the pith, which they use to make their enchanting music.

As Adder Stones, Holey Stones were revered by Druids and some were carried as a kind of Druidic badge of office[66]. They also appear in the ancient Welsh legend of *Peredur, Son of Efrawg* when Peredur is given a magical stone that helps him to see and kill an invisible monster[67] and in *The Lady of the Fountain* when Owain is gifted such a stone by a Faerie maiden. It makes him invisible and allows him to escape from a castle[68].

Holed Fairy Stones can also provide a home or shelter for Faerie beings. With its link to Odin and the breath of life and the fact that air can pass freely through Holed Stones, means that they are firm favourites with the Faeries of Air known as Sylphs who love playing in and around them. In Russia Holey Stones were placed around the home and chicken coop to provide homes for the Faeries known as Kurinyi Bog ('the Chicken God') and the Kikimora, who were female House Sprites, while at the same time keeping away any malevolent Sprites.

Holed Stones can help us to breathe life into new projects and to liven up our relationship with the Fae. They encourage us to look to the Faeries for advice and to speak to them about our hopes and dreams. Remember, 'Everything that comes to you, comes to teach you.' The Faeries have much to teach us if we are willing to listen. These stones can be valuable conduits of communication with the Faeries, allowing us to communicate with them and allowing them to communicate with us in meditation or trance-like states when we use our mind's eye, inner eye or Third Eye to psychically 'see' the messages and symbols that the Faeries have for us. They can also help us to see through any barriers or obstacles that might be preventing us working with the Faeries, such as our own fears, a lack of confidence or our egos. The holes also allow only good Faeries to communicate with us and only allow us to communicate with the Faeries when we do so for the higher good, in this way they protect everyone involved.

Fairy Stones (Calcite)

Other Names: Venus Stone or Concretions
Chemical Composition: Varies, but often something like $CaCO_3$
Element: Earth
Season: All
Planet: Earth and Mars
Chakra: Earth Star
Birthstone: Birthstone for all Faerie Beings
Faerie Monarchs/Deities: Venus, all Earth Mothers such as Gaia, Terra, Jord, Nerthus, Mawu, PachaMama and Danu
Faeries: They are their own type of Faerie

Fairy Stones are wonderfully strange bulbous stones that are essentially Clay, Sand and Silt with minerals such as Calcite, Hematite and Pyrite in them that are consolidated by a Limestone cement. These concretions can be found in a wide variety of rocks, though they are most commonly found in Sandstone, Shale and Silt deposits. They are found in many places on Earth and also on Mars. The Martian ones are known as Martian Spherules or Blueberries. The name Concretion derives from the Latin *con* – 'together' and *crescere* – 'to grow'. They have a randomness to them that reminds us of the randomness in everything and a kind of cheekiness that highlights the playful, mischievous nature of Faerie beings. In their randomness, they vary in hardness, size, shape, colour, making each stone unique, just as every human and every Faerie is unique. We all come in various shapes, sizes and colours; this is to be celebrated and not used to discriminate in any way.

It was originally the Indigenous Algonquians of North America who called these stones 'Fairy Stones'. They were carried by hunters and fishermen to bring them luck and bounty.

Lovers would exchange Fairy Stones as tokens of their affection and many would be kept in pride of place in the home to bring good fortune and at the same time to keep away malevolent spirits and bad luck. *We can still bring them into our homes for this same purpose today.*

Some say that these odd looking little stones act as talismans to bring Faerie blessings to the home, while other say that these really are small helpful Faeries who are turned to stone by the rays of the Sun as described in many old folk tales. The important difference is that these Faeries, unlike those that now form stone menhirs and monuments for whom the change was permanent, can transform back into their Faerie form once the Sun goes down. So in bringing a Calcite Fairy Stone into your life and your home, you are literally bringing in a nocturnal Faerie Being. That said, they apparently find us when they feel that we are ready to work with and befriend them rather than us finding them.

If a Fairy Stone chooses to come into your life, make sure you keep it somewhere where it can do its thing in peace. They much prefer to be kept out in pride of place, such as on display or on your Faerie altar, rather than being put in a drawer or box, so they can fly free at night without disturbing you or anyone else in your home. They will watch over you and your home in the night, and you can ask them to keep away bad dreams and bad energies that might otherwise disturb you. They can soothe and smooth away our worries and have a very calming influence.

These Faeries help us to connect to the Earth and all her energies and to sacred power places such as the great stone circles, the pyramids, the Isle of Avalon, and to the few magical Faerie Forests that still exist. Perhaps this is why they often resemble those Mother Earth Goddess figures of Limestone and Calcite from Palaeolithic times that we refer to as Venuses, or Venus figurines, such as the renowned Venus of Willendorf, the Venus of Moravany, the Venus of Mal'ta, the Venus of Hohle

Fehls and the disputed Venus of Orkney. These figures, like Fairy Stones, are of the Earth and represent the fertility and energies of our Earth Mother. They keep us in the here and now, centring and balancing our energies. Fairy Stones, the Venuses and the Earth Mothers from myths and legends show us the plentiful bounty of the Earth and educate us that we have to give back to the Earth in order to help keep her healthy and happy. Here we are reminded to recycle and to compost what we can and to tread lightly upon the body of our mother. Fairy Stones assist us in working through and healing any issues we have with the Earth, with motherhood, our own mortal mothers and our own children. Even if we are childless these wonderful Faerie companions highlight to us that we are mothers in other ways, for we might birth works of creativity and can still share our knowledge and skills with others. When Faerie Stones come into our lives they do so as an act of love and they show us that our Mother Earth or Mother Goddess (whoever you like to think of as your Cosmic Mother) loves us very much.

As stones are the bones of the Earth and our bones are formed from calcium (Calcite is a form of calcium) in folklore and traditional folk medicine Fairy Stones have long been carried by people with problems with their bones, such as rickets or arthritis.

These Faeries make excellent allies and friends, helping us in many ways, but in particular with our magical work. They love to help us to create a safe space for our magical workings such as a sacred circle or Faerie Ring and work hard to make our homes safe, secure and happy spaces for us to live in. Fairy Stones are adept at guiding us and protecting us during meditations that connect us with the Earth or that take us down into the Deep Earth realms where the Dwarves and Gnomes live.

Like us, every Fairy Stone is completely unique and will have its own personality, its own temperament, its own skills and likes/dislikes. If you are lucky enough to have a Fairy

Stone companion come into your life, make them feel welcome, befriend them and find out who they are for yourself. Then they will reveal what they have to share with you and what they would like you to share with them. Have fun and know that you are very blessed!

Calcite is very soft and it easily scratched, so please do take care when handling and storing these lovely stones.

Fluorite

Other Names: Fluorspar, Rainbow Stone, Blue John or Derbyshire Spar
Chemical Composition: CaF_2
Element: Magic and Spirit
Season: Spring
Planet: Venus
Chakra: Third Eye
Birthstone: Capricorn and Pisces
Other: State Mineral of Illinois, Regional Mineral for Central England and County Stone for Derbyshire
Faerie Monarchs/Deities: Heimdall, Iris, Queen Mab/Maeve, Mbaba Mwana Waresa, Yolgni and all deities associated with rainbows
Faeries: The Faeries of the Rainbow. The Faeries of Sleep like La Dormette and the Sandman Also some Flower Faeries and Anthousai of purple flowers including heather, lavender, irises, purple coneflower, asters and passionflower

A popular stone, especially for those just entering the world of crystals, as it has a very gentle, soft energy that is perfect for children or beginners. Often used as an alternative to the more potent Amethyst, Fluorite is also very protective and a very Faerie stone. It is reputed to protect us from all negative energies such as bad vibes, ill wishing, jealousy and electro-magnetic radiation. Its name comes from the Latin *fluere* meaning 'to flow' as Fluorite was used in iron smelting to improve the fluidity of the iron slag to make it easier to process.

Fluorite is a crystal for the sensitive and psychic soul, for it is the stone of sensitivity and psychic awareness. Fluorite sensitises us to the world around us, to its energies and to the Faeries and other souls that are living alongside us, allowing us to see, hear and communicate with them. Fluorite sensitises you to others and their needs, but it also stops us from becoming too sensitive or oversensitive. It stabilises our psychic abilities and emotions, putting us firmly back in control over our emotions and our life. It can also help us to become sensitive to the energies around us in terms of being able to sense people's energies, Auras, energies of place and the Energy Lines in the landscape. Many people can do this with the help of pendulums and other energy tools, but Fluorite is keen to point out that those items are tools to make the process easier. With time and practice we can heighten our sensitivities so that we no longer need the tools, because we can do it alone as the ability was ours all along.

Fluorite brings structure to the disorganised mind, bringing with it spiritual, mental and psychological stability and clarity. It awakens our spirituality and our soul via our Third Eye Chakra. It also operates on a practical level, enhancing our discernment and our common sense. Fluorite brings self-control through understanding ourselves and who we are. In meditation or dream work Fluorite will take you away with the Faeries and bring you safely back again. Importantly it enables you to bring what you have learned from the Faeries into your life in a spiritual and very practical way. Fluorite assists us in contemplation or meditation, helping us to reflect in peace and with our full range of senses and abilities to really dig deep with our introspection and self-searching. It aligns our conscious and subconscious minds, promoting deep understanding and crystal-clear thinking.

One of Fluorite's most important lessons for us is the importance of not taking things too personally. It trains us in how to give and take constructive criticism gracefully and to learn from it. It supports you when you feel hurt in any way, soothing the pain, encouraging forgiveness and bringing you a sense of peace. Fluorite is a very useful stone for twenty-first century life; it is thought to help us cope better with stresses and ever-tightening deadlines.

Fluorite comes in many colours, literally a whole rainbow of colours from clear to green, blue, purple, yellow, pink and brown. You may be lucky enough to meet a stone with many colours all in one. As it comes in so many beautiful hues it is closely linked with the rainbow and the Gods and Goddesses of the rainbow and the rainbow as a bridge connecting our world to the Faerie Otherworld. Iris, the Greek personification of the rainbow, brought messages from the Gods and Goddesses to us in our dreams via her rainbow. We can call on Iris to bring and belay our messages to the Divine and to Faerie. In a similar vein Queen Mab of British Faerielore was also renowned for midwifing dreams and visions into our realm from the Faerie Otherworld. We can ask Mab to protect us while we sleep and to bring us meaningful dreams and messages from the Fae in our dreams and visions. Mab may also assist us with spirit journeying in our dreams, escorting us to and from her castle in Faerieland, or anywhere else in any realm, as in Shelley's *Queen Mab; A Philosophical Poem*[69]. With its ability to gently lull us to sleep, Fluorite is linked with the Faeries of Sleep such as the French La Dormette, the Danish Ole Luk Øj and the Sandman who sprinkles dust into our eyes to get us to sleep – hence why we wake up with 'sleep' in our eyes.

Just as Heimdall, the Guardian of the Bifrost Rainbow Bridge connecting Earth to Heaven in Norse legend, could hear the grass growing in the fields and see at night as if it were day even a hundred leagues away[70], Fluorite encourages us to also develop our senses – although perhaps not quite to the extent that Heimdall has done. Fluorite can be used to heal, hone and heighten our physical senses of touch, taste, sight, hearing and smell and our more metaphysical senses such as our sixth sense and the clairs – *clairvoyance* – 'clear seeing', *clairsentience* – 'clear feeling', *clairaudience* – 'clear hearing', and *claircognisance* – 'clear knowing'. It increases our awareness and our ability to engage with others on a whole new level. Fluorite shows us that we can trust these senses, our intuition and our gut feelings.

With its link with all purple flowers, Fluorite connects us to the magical world of the Flower Faeries and the Anthousai (Flower Nymphs) who lovingly tend our pot plants and garden plants as well as wildflowers. The Flower Faeries teach us how to garden effectively for beauty and for our fellow creatures as many species of birds and bugs are now highly reliant on our gardens as sources of food and shelter. We can ask the Flower Faeries for guidance on which plants to buy, when and where to plant our plants and how to take good care of them. In the same way these gentle Faeries can also show us how to take better care of ourselves too. When we bloom or our flowers bloom as a result of their care and advice we should always show our gratitude to these wonderful Faeries, thereby building up an inspirational and enchanting relationship.

In particular, Fluorite is associated with the beautiful flowers of heather that come in a variety of whites, lilacs and purples. The term *Heathen* for those who work with the Old Norse and Germanic Gods derives from heather and heathland. Heather's Latin name, *Calluna vulgaris,* derives from the Greek *kallyno* (καλλύνω), meaning 'to beautify' or to 'sweep clean'. In times past heather was used in besoms to sweep stagnant energies as well dirt out of the house and sweep positive energies in. In many ways this is also how Fluorite works, cleansing away old or negative energies and bringing in beautiful new positive energies. Heather was also said to bring sweet and deeply spiritual dreams and visions, like those that Queen Mab brings us.

Traditionally Fluorite was used to relieve pain of all kinds, especially emotional and spiritual pain or anguish. It cleanses the Aura and has a wonderfully regenerative effect. In times past it was used for healing wounds to the mind, body or soul. Purple fluorite was used for all kinds of spiritual healing, pink Fluorite was to heal matters of the heart, green Fluorite was used to heal disorders of the bones, teeth and hair and to sooth arthritis and blue Fluorite was used for communication issues, coughs and colds.

Fluorite mined in the UK may also be known as Blue John or Derbyshire Spar for there is a source of a highly prized and rather decorative Fluorite in Derbyshire, which has been sent out all over the world. Blue John has a very lovely blue to purple tone with bands of clear, white or yellow running through it.

Fluorite and its Faeries encourage us to take time out of the everyday to rest, recuperate and reflect. They assist us in avoiding distractions, prioritising our time effectively and enabling us to find time away from others to focus on self-healing and self-development without being selfish. Fluorite shows us how to be comfortable with solitude and to be able to enjoy our own company. We cannot effectively give to others if we have nothing in us to give, so Fluorite shows us that through healing ourselves we are in fact helping to heal others too.

Many samples of Fluorite exhibit mild fluorescence under ultraviolet light, hence why the effect is named after the mineral. Fluorescence shows us light in the darkness, a light we might not otherwise see, so is a handy reminder for us to sense and acknowledge the light and soul within all things, even if we cannot see it and to know that there is always a light at the end of the tunnel.

Calcite is very soft and it easily scratched, so please do take care when wearing, handling or storing Fluorite.

Garnet

Other Names: Carbuncle, Gooseberry Stone, Pomegranate Stone, the Stone of Warriors or Elie Ruby

Chemical Composition: $A_3B_2Si_3O_{12}$, where A is a Fe^{2+}, Ca^{2+}, Mg^{2+}, Mn^{2+} and B is Fe^{3+}, Al^{3+}, Cr^{3+}

Element: Earth and Fire

Season: Summer

Planet: Mars and Jupiter

Chakra: Base

Birthstone: January, Aquarius, Aries, Leo and Sagittarius

Anniversary: The second wedding anniversary

Other: Day Stone for Tuesdays, Regional Stone of the Fife area, State Mineral of Connecticut, State Gemstone of New York and Vermont, Stone of Bohemia

Faerie Monarchs/Deities: Queen Mab/Maeve, King Arthur and Brân the Blessed

Faeries: Djinn, Fire Sprites and Salamanders

There are two theories as to where Garnet gets its name: one is that it comes from the Latin *granate* meaning 'seed' due to the stone's likeness to the seed of the pomegranate, while the other theory is that it derives from the Old English *gernet* meaning 'dark red'. As with Carnelian, its gentler companion, this fruit connection means that Garnet has been used to traditionally treat stomach disorders and to assist with the absorption of nutrients.

Garnet is a gloriously deep dark red stone with a very vital and enlivening energy. It symbolises pure, primal and potent power. Garnet demonstrates how power and energy can be positive or negative – it is how we use it that matters. It also reminds us of the need to be both strong and adaptable in order to survive.

All red stones, in particular Garnets and Rubies, are highly prized. On a carat for carat basis Rubies are more valuable than Diamonds! In Scotland there's a legend that red stones were *Fuil Siochare ('Faerie Blood Stones') that fell from the Faerie Battles in the skies that caused the Northern Lights*[71]. *Because blood was thought to be a very powerful substance and retain the energy of its owner, any such red stones* were highly sought after for their magical properties. As Garnet has the appearance of solidified blood, it has long been traditionally used to treat all kinds of blood disorders such as anaemia, circulation problems and heart disease, and to stop bleeding and heal wounds. Naturally, this should never replace proper healthcare.

Garnets are among the red stones found in Scotland. Ruby Bay, near Elie in Fife, is a bit of a misnomer as it is Garnets not Rubies that are found there, hence the alternative name for Garnet of Elie Ruby[72]. Elsewhere in Scottish folklore there's mention of the *Clach Dearg* ('Red Stone') that added healing power to water and *to the Lee Penny, a heart-shaped red gemstone that was reputed to cure haemorrhage, fever and pestilence*[73].

Garnet is the stone of warriors, and amulets of it were particularly popular with warriors and soldiers in ancient and more recent conflicts as it supposedly helped protect them in battle. It was also used in times past to staunch and heal wounds (don't try that at home). While Labradorite is the stone of the spiritual warrior, Garnet is the stone of the physical and mental warrior, helping us to overcome obstacles such as our fears, our doubts, any lack in confidence or esteem, and any other negative programming we have picked up that sabotages us inside. Garnet wants us to see ourselves as survivors rather than victims because it wishes for us to take back our power. The Ogham Stave Fearn – the alder – connects to Garnet as a stone of protection. The alder is sacred to the Welsh Faerie and Warrior King Brân who defended Britain from invaders in life and in death. After he was poisoned, Brân asked for his head to be buried beneath what is now the site of the Tower of London, facing out to the continent, so that he could continue to protect the British Isles. Brân, like Arthur, is a Once and Future King. Garnets were also popular with Saxon Warriors and Kings, several important parts of the Sutton Hoo treasure, such as the purse lid, shoulder clasps and most importantly the warrior's sword, feature extraordinarily ornate and beautiful Garnet cloisonné cell work[74].

Garnet is a very powerful stone whose energy can be felt at quite a distance from the actual crystal, just as the heat from a hearth fire can be felt a few feet away. Indeed it has that same fiery energy to it, like the roaring flames of a smith's furnace or a hearth fire, and Fire Sprites and Salamanders are drawn to its energy just as they are to flames. If you are a fiery or passionate soul or born below a fire sign then you will adore its energies. Here it is also worth noting that the Sutton Hoo warrior also had rough Garnets in a pouch along with a fire steel, perhaps they were a charm to assist with fire lighting?

Holding a Garnet when you feel lethargic or run down in any way will inspire and fire up your energy levels, for Garnet has an energising, uplifting and vital energy. It is a stone of dynamism, of making things happen and making changes. Changes are inevitable in life and Garnet instructs us to seize the day and make the most of any changes. Helping us to overcome crises and mishaps, Garnet keeps us looking forward. Sharing its get-up-and-go energy with us, it encourages us to forge ahead no matter what. If you are recovering from an illness Garnet can help restore your energy levels and life force, bringing a renewed sense of vitality and optimism. It boosts the human energy system and fires up the fiery balls of energy that are our Chakras, cleansing and revitalising them at the same time.

It is an ideal companion stone for the modern manager or leader as it encourages leadership qualities of the kind where we lead by example, inspiring and encouraging others. It is a stone of order and stability, so is ideal to have nearby when you are making plans that will affect your career or health. It is also a great stone for the entrepreneur or for the self-employed forging their own career in their own way as it is associated with prosperity and success too. Traditionally Garnet amulets and charms have been utilised by those working in the legal sector or when fighting legal cases. Often used for manifestation work, it realises our dreams and in times past was used to prevent nightmares.

Associated with the Base Chakra, Garnet is a stone of sensuality, sexuality, passion, love, fertility and energy. It enhances our fertility and creativity on all levels. It is ideal for those who want to create anything, be it a baby or an epic novel. The stone is very beneficial to mothers/fathers-to-be and new mums/dads or anyone whose energy and hormone levels are depleted. Rich, red Garnet teaches us to enjoy our earthly lives in all ways and make the most of our time on this physical plane. Garnet enables us to find our passions in life and to be passionate about the things we care about. Inspiring love in all its many forms, it shows us how to love life, love ourselves and to love others. Garnet and its associated Faeries are very upbeat; they encourage us to have a positive outlook. In times past it was used to treat depression, melancholy or any form of 'the blues' as Garnet's deep red is at the other end of the colour wheel.

Garnet is a powerful stone of friendship and can fire up friendships that have been waning due to things like time and physical distance. Garnet encourages friendships between all species and beings, especially with our animal companions and our Faerie companions. Garnets are linked with wishes and hopes and are watched over by Djinn, the Genies of Ancient Arabia, who grant wishes and were created from smokeless fire. As always, we must be careful as to what we wish for...

Should you find the energy of Garnet a little overwhelming, Carnelian is a very useful alternative.

Granite

Chemical Composition: Potassium feldspar ($KAlSi_3O_8$) Plagioclase Feldspar ($NaAlSi_3O_8$ to $CaAl_2Si_2O_8$) and Quartz (SiO_2) differing amounts of Muscovite ($KAl_2(AlSi_3O_{10})$ $(F,OH)_2$), Biotite ($K(Mg,Fe)$ $3(AlSi3O10)(F,OH)2$ $3O10)$ (F,OH)) and Hornblende-type amphiboles (($(Ca,Na)_{2-3}(Mg,Fe,Al)_5(Al,Si)_8O_{22}(OH,F)_2$)

Element: Deep Earth

Season: All, but especially winter

Planet: Earth

Chakra: Earth Star and Soul Star

Other: State Stone of New Hampshire, which is also called the Granite State and State Stone of North Carolina and Vermont. Unofficially a county stone for Cornwall and Devon

Faerie Monarchs/Deities: Fionn mac Cumhaill

Faeries: Pixies, Trows, Trolls, Gnomes, Devas, Salamanders, Oreads, Giants and Djinn

The name Granite comes from the Latin word for 'grain' – *granum* due to its coarse granular appearance. It is from its grains that it obtains much of its beauty, for while granite comes in various grey, white, red and even pink hues, it gets extra colour and sparkle from its Mica, Feldspar and Quartz particulates. This mish-mash effect is a beautiful reminder of how the disparate can be brought together to create something magical. Meditating with Granite helps us to bring all the different aspects of our lives and ourselves together in harmony and helps us to feel as if we're keeping it together, even if you're getting drawn in many different directions.

Found all over planet Earth, but apparently only on planet Earth, Granite is the Rock of Ages. Granite is essentially the calm, cooled, solidified magma left behind after all the drama of the volcano so can help us find calm, healing and peace after traumatic events. Its origins give Granite both a fiery energy and a deeply earthy energy, meaning it is a favourite of all Fire and Earth-associated Faeries such as Salamanders and Gnomes.

Granite is incredibly hard, tough and dense. It teaches us toughness, but tempers any hardness of heart with compassion. It is a stone of formation and foundation, and is often used for foundation stones of buildings, showing us the importance of building deep and strong foundations for our ventures if we wish them to last. Granite is a stone of longevity and legacy. Granite buildings and monuments have lasted well through the ages, despite weathering from the elements showing that we too, with Granite's guidance, can weather storms and persevere no matter what life throws our way. This is why Granite is a very popular stone for memorials and gravestones, in order to ensure a lasting legacy. Granite is also renowned for its ability to connect the Heavens and Earth through its energies and structure. It grounds spiritual energy yet raises the vibrations of the physical so that the two can comfortably meet in the middle. It was used to build Ancient Egyptian and Indian temples, places where the earthly and Divine meet, and was used to make the capstone for the Black Pyramid of Amenemhat III[75] and the huge sarcophagus and King's Chamber within the Great Pyramid of Giza[76].

Granite epitomises the psyche and the soul of the land in which it is found. The energies of Granite vary from place to place, as does it colour and chemical composition. Its energies are also influenced by its landscape and the cultures and peoples that have developed around it. Pink Aswan Granite from Egypt, which was often used for columns and obelisks, enables us to connect to the fiery Djinn or Genies of the Egyptian deserts, who like Granite were born of fire, and to the energy and wisdom of Ancient Egypt and its Deities. With its pink hue Aswan Granite connects with us through our Heart Chakra and teaches us of compassion and reverence. Indian granite with its more grounding and centring energy connects us to the wisdom and mysteries of India and the Devic World. Grey Granite from Granite Bay in California has a more cerebral and contemplative energy that encourages us to look out on the world and to look within at the same time, connecting the inner with the outer aspects of our existence. Grey Granite from Britain connects us to the Neolithic and Celtic Cultures of the British Isles, to their places of power that were made from Granite or used Granite outcrops, and to the many Faeries connected with Granite. There's a famous, craggy island of Granite in the Outer Firth of Clyde known as *Ailse Craig* meaning 'Faerie Rock'. As with every hill and mountain, Ailse Craig has its own *Oread* – a 'Nymph or Faerie of a Mountain'.

It is also possible to find white Granite – white being a very Faerie colour indeed – and white Granite connects us to the energies of the stars, the Moon and the spiritual plane. On the Isle of Arran there are two stunning and highly visible white Granite stone circles (numbers 4 and 5) to be found at Machrie Moor, and a third (number 1) has alternating Granite and Sandstone stones. According to local legends the many stone circles of Machrie Moor were made by Fairies or Giants sitting on nearby Durra-na-each Mountain and flicking 'pebbles' onto the moor below[77]. Another legend about stone circle number 5 at Machrie Moor connects it to the Irish hero and Giant Fionn mac Cumhaill, who is credited with creating the Giant's Causeway and who encountered many Faeries in his mythical adventures, for it is also known as *Suidh Coire Fhionn* or 'Fingal's Cauldron Seat'[78]. It's worth noting here that *Fionn*, and *Gwynn*, his Welsh variant, both share a name meaning 'White'.

Pixies love Granite and its sparkles. The Granite tors, standing stones and dolmens of Cornwall and Devon are well known as Pixie haunts, some are even named after them like Pixie's Parlour, Pixies' House and Pixies' Church. The three stones of Mên-an-Tol, the two upright and the holed stone, are all made from Granite. Local legends tell that Mên-an-Tol is home to a very benevolent Pixie who would cure all sorts of ills if a human passed through the magical hole in the central stone. In many ways this Holed Stone was a portal into Faerieland provided access to its healing powers, it was even said that if a Changeling was passed into the hole, the human baby would be what came out the other side[79]. Granite in any form, and its Guardian Faeries, can also assist us with healing and making ourselves whole. Other sites, like the Granite tor known as the Cheesewring, are associated with Giants; another name for it was 'The Giant's House'. The story goes that the outcrop is the result of a stone-throwing competition between a mighty Giant and a frail saint. Many Granite outcrops all over Europe are said to be Trolls or Giants that stayed out too long and were turned to stone by the first rays of dawn sunlight. The Granite rocks of Orkney and Shetland are also popular resting places for the local Trows, who are like diminutive and more benevolent Trolls with a deep love for music.

Faeries are drawn to Granite because it reminds them of many of their homes and sacred sites. Placing Granite in your home, garden or on your Faerie altar can help them to feel a little more at home and at ease with you. Granite can be used to create modern sacred stone circles within your home or garden, providing a ritual space or a space away from the everyday. Granite connects us to sacred sites all over the world, to the currents of energy that crisscross all over our planet and to the Earth's magnetic field. It can also teach us the intricacies of our own energy systems. With its fine detail and granular appearance, Granite can assist us in any work that requires detail and accuracy; it literally gets us down to the nitty-gritty. Traditionally Granite has been used to treat cellular and immune system disorders, and any other disorders where the ability to see/hear/comprehend details has been lost, such as the loss of sight, hearing and memory problems.

Granite encourages trust and peace between different peoples, cultures and between humans and other beings like Faeries, but it only does so when that trust is deserved and can be built upon as a solid foundation. Because it links our Earth Star and Soul Star Chakras, Granite helps us to feel comfortable being a spiritual being in a physical body, it firmly grounds us to Mother Earth, but also encourages us to reach up to the Heavens and our Star Father above. When meditating it provides a concrete and stabilising bridge so that while our bodies remain firmly in the here and now, our spirits can safely journey into the beyond and back again. A stone of perseverance and endurance, Granite gives us strength and connects us to the strength and stability of the Earth and the power of the stars while reminding us of our many duties and responsibilities in and to the world. It helps us not to feel too overwhelmed by our lives and all that is going on around us, but centres us in the midst of it all in peace, as if we are in the eye of the storm.

If you ever feel that your personal or spiritual development is on hold due to the commitments and practicalities of life, meditate and work with Granite and its Faeries to find ways to bring the spiritual into the everyday so that you can continue to develop and evolve.

Jet

Other Names: Garnet of Elie Ruby Black Amber, Witches' Stone/Witch's Stone, Lignite, Jess, Gagates or Sea-Coal. When mined in Whitby it is known as Whitby Jet and when mined in Turkey is called Oltu Stone
Element: Deep Earth, Wood, Spirit and Cosmos
Season: Winter
Planet: None, rather this is the darkness of the Cosmos
Chakra: Base
Birthstone: Capricorn, Scorpio and January
Other: Regional stone for the North-East of England, especially the town of Whitby
Faerie Monarchs/Deities: Gwynn ap Nudd, Mani, Gwydion, Epona/Rhiannon, The Cailleach and The Morríghan
Faeries: Dryads and Tree Sprites, especially those of the 'darker' trees such as the aspen or yew and of the deeper less reachable parts of large forests. Also associated with the Ballybog and Greencoaties

Like Amber, Jet was once part of ancient trees, for it is formed under immense pressures from decaying ancient wood. It is a form of Lignite and a forerunner to Coal. Jet is a very beautiful soft dark brown or black in colour, reminiscent of the enveloping blackness of the dark skies against which the stars twinkle. Occasionally Jet can contain sparkle too in the form of golden Pyrite inclusions, but mostly it is consistently dark in colour. The word Jet comes from the French word *jaiet*, which in turn comes from the Greek name of Γαγάτης ◉(Gagátēs), all of which refer to this lovely mineraloid[80]. It is from Jet that we get the term 'Jet-Black' for anything that is very deep black in colour. As white is the presence of all the colours, black is the absence of colour and you really do get the sense of that with Jet, which seems to absorb all the colours and all our worries into its deep abyss. Traditionally due to this Jet has been used to draw off and absorb anxiety, aches and pains and negative energies.

As Moonstone is the stone of the energies of the Full Moon, Jet is the stone of the Waxing and Dark Moon, which holds all that energy of potential within its darkness. As with Moonstone, Jet can be very helpful for all hormone issues, especially those that affect our monthly cycles and our biorhythms. Jet is particularly powerful around the time of Samhain and the Winter Solstice – the Longest Night of the Year. It represents the stillness of the in-between, whether that is in terms of energies or times of the day or year. Although Jet is easy to carve, it is also very easy to break, showing us the need to be gentle and caring with ourselves and others, especially during times of transition. Jet is the perfect stone to accompany us through times of change and transformation. It teaches us acceptance and supports us through endings and conclusions while at the same time preparing us for the new starts and rebirth that are sure to follow. Jet and its Faeries support us through loss and grief with a very deep level of compassion. This is possibly part of why Jet has been so popular as mourning jewellery for more than a hundred years, a trend that started with Queen Victoria after the death of her husband, Prince Albert.

Jet's organic origins mean that it is a stone that combines the energies of the Earth, Nature – particularly trees, and Spirit. Jet is the dark twin of Amber and in modern Wicca and Witchcraft many priests and priestesses like to wear necklaces of Jet and Amber, hence Jet's nickname of the Witches' Stone. When worn in this way the Jet represents darkness, night time and the Dark Deities and Faerie Monarchs like Gwynn ap Nudd and Gwydion and Amber is day, the light and the Deities of Light such as Sol and Lugh. In the Faerie Tradition Amber is the stone of the Summer Faerie Queens, or the Summer Faces of the Goddess, like Áine and Brighid while Jet is the stone of the Winter Faerie

Queens or Winter Faces of the Goddess like Gráinne and The Cailleach. Jet is also the stone of the Dark Irish Goddess and Faerie Queen, The Morríghan, who would transform herself into the form of a jet-black crow.

Like Amber, Jet has been used and worn as a talisman for millennia. Those who are drawn to Jet are thought to be old souls or natural magicians and witches who have been incarnated on this Earth many times and have worked with Faeries and other magical beings in many lives. With its softly reflective sheen it was thought to drive away evil and protect you from the evil eye[81]. In times past Jet was thought to protect people from thunder, to drive out Demons and snakes[82], and to chase away malevolent Spirits or Sprites. It is a strongly protective stone and deflects the negativity of others away from you, which helps to keep your energy system clear and functional. With its soft, soothing energy, Jet makes a good worry stone in times of stress and can be placed under the bed to bring a good night's sleep. As it is light in the hand, Jet enables us to effortlessly float in the sweet, soft oblivion of sleep and to rise above anxieties that weigh us down. It is a lovely material to meditate with and very tactile, partly because Jet feels warm to the touch, and Jet beads are very popular for Catholic rosaries and Pagan prayer beads. Long strings of jet beads were also the height of fashion in the 1920s.

Jet is linked with the Faeries of the deeper, less accessible parts of the forest where most humans simply do not go. Jet is also associated with those Dryads and Tree Sprites who inhabit trees with darker reputations in folklore, such as the whispering aspen and the yew. These are not sinister trees or beings, just perhaps less well understood. They are still wise and wondrous, but few have dared or bothered to accept them for what they truly are. Aspen was also closely linked with Annwn – the Welsh Underworld or Otherworld from where the Faery Queen Rhiannon/Epona originated – and with her partner, Pywll who was known as the King of Annwn. Aspen was considered unlucky because measuring sticks – used to measure up for coffins – were made of its wood, but it could also be very lucky too as shields were made from it that could literally save a warrior's life. Yew is another tree linked with death, but it also has the ability to rebirth itself as its branches grow down into the ground to form new stems, which then rise up around the old central growth as separate but linked trunks. This is the lesson of these darker trees: that death is nothing to fear, nor is the unknown for from death comes new life and renewal.

Jet is also connected to the Ballybog Faeries who live in areas of peatland and serve as guardians of the peat. In the past the Ballybogs and humans did not get on because mankind dug up so much peat, destroying their homes, but today they are generally friendly to humans as long as we respect their peaty homeland. Naturally these muddy Faeries are very keen to get us to use peat-free compost in our gardening and in doing so we can become firm friends with these creatures. Jet is also loved by the Greencoaties or Tiddy Mun of the Fens who dwelt in bogs and had powers over the waters before the Fens were drained. They still live in the Fens today, in the more remote areas where they look after nature, the waters and the harvests.

Jet emphasises our need to sometimes get back to basics, to focus on the essentials and to re-evaluate what is important. Jet encourages us to effectively deal with the demands made of us by others and by ourselves so can be very handy for perfectionists. Helping us to overcome disappointments, Jet reminds us of the lessons that failures, regret and setbacks have for us. Jet shows us how to safely and positively assert ourselves, teaching us to be firm and resolute.

Traditionally it is used in magical workings to enhance psychic awareness as it opens us to both the deep, ancient mysteries of the Earth and the timeless mysteries of the cosmos. Many who perform readings or divination will wear Jet or have a Jet stone close by to provide added depth to their readings and to enhance the messages that they bring. Jet is a stone of communication, especially communication between the world of the living and the dead, not in terms of mediumship, but more that it helps to convey love between loved ones who are still alive and those who have passed over.

Jet often washes up on the shores of North-East England, which is why the Saxons called it 'Sea-Coal' and it has long been mined in the Whitby area. Whitby Jet is some of the finest and most famous in the world. I cannot help thinking the influence and magic of Jet in the Whitby area had something to do with Bram Stoker's *Dracula*. Abraham (Bram) Stoker was inspired by St Mary's churchyard in Whitby, Yorkshire, to write *Dracula* and in his book, Whitby is where Count Dracula landed when he first came to England. Many consider Jet a very Gothic stone, with its heady mix of romance and darkness.

Jet is well known to absorb the energies of its owner or wearer so please use Jet only for yourself, never on anyone else. Jet needs regular cleansing and enjoys being cleansed and recharged beneath the New Moon.

Labradorite

Other Names: Spectrolite, Madagascar Moonstone, Aurora Stone, Labrador Moonstone, Labrador Feldspar or Carnatite

Chemical Composition: $Na(AlSi_3O_8)Ca(Al_2Si_2O_8)$

Element: Ice, Magic, Spirit and Cosmos

Season: Winter

Planet: The Sun

Chakra: Soul Star

Birthstone: Birthstone of all us with a magical soul, especially for those born in the darker times of the year when the Northern Lights/Southern Lights can be seen more clearly, so October, November and December for those born in the Northern Hemisphere and for those born in May, June and July in the Southern Hemisphere

Other: Stone of the Labrador area

Faerie Monarchs/Deities: Freyja, The Cailleach and Aurora

Faeries: Elves, the Sidhe, the Valkyries, the Aurora Faeries, the Perry Men and the Merry Men

Labradorite is a stone of pure magic and magical power like no other stone on this Earth. It is a deeply spiritual stone that works with us down to the deepest and most ancient parts of our very soul. Labradorite takes the light of the cosmos and the Divine into the darkest depths to cleanse, heal and inspire. On first glance Labradorite can look like a mundane grey or green rock, but when the light catches it at the right angle that is when the magic is revealed. The lesson here is that sometimes to really see what is going on or to reveal the magic we have to change our perspective. According to tradition this magical light can help fill the holes in our Aura, healing it and helping us to shine.

Labradorite is named after Labrador in Canada, where it was

first found. It is also found in Finland where it shows a broader spectrum of colours in its flash, hence when mined in Finland it is called Spectrolite. Both Labrador and Finland are areas where the Northern Lights can often be seen weaving and flashing their way across the skies. There is a beautiful Inuit myth about Labradorite: the Northern Lights had been imprisoned in the rocks of Labrador until an Inuit warrior found them and sought to free them with his spear. He was not able to free all of the light so some still remains trapped in the rocks to this day where they flash and shine in response to the Aurora above.

Even the term *Aurora* has a Faerie connection. The name *Aurora Borealis* was coined in 1621CE by Pierre Gassendi who chose to name the phenomena after Boreas, the Greek God of the North Wind (who is often depicted with bird or Faerie-like wings) and after Aurora, the Roman Faerie Goddess of the Dawn, who renews herself every morning and flies across the sky.

There are many stories from all over the world about what or who causes the Northern and Southern Lights that dance across the sky above our planet's two polar regions. In Finland the lights are said to be caused by snow and ice churned up by the bushy tail of an Arctic fox as it runs across the tundra. In Canada and Greenland the lights were the fires of the souls of the dead or of Giants who lived in the High Arctic. In Scandinavia the lights were thought to be the wake of Freya's great chariot, which was drawn by two lynxes, or by the weapons, shields and chariots of the Valkyries[83], the takers of the slain, who are akin to Faerie Women. Some say that the lights are the Bifrost, the Rainbow Bridge that connects the land of man to the land of the Gods. In the far North the lights were well respected and there were many taboos about what you could or could not do while the lights were dancing above you. This highlights even today that magic and the power of nature are to be respected.

In Ireland the Northern Lights were said to result from the revels of the Sidhe, and the colours and patterns were formed by

the swishing of their incandescent robes. In William Allingham's poem *The Fairies*, the Old Faerie King of the poem is said to be:
...Going up with music

On cold starry nights
To sup with the Queen
Of the gay Northern Lights.

In Scotland the lights were called the Merry Dancers or *Fir Chlis* ('Nimble Men') and the Aurora was the result of the dancing of these Nimble Men and Merry Maidens who were Faerie beings enjoying Faerie revels[84]. However, there was also a darker side to the Aurora, which reminds us that magic and indeed all forms of energy can be used for good or bad. The story goes that there were two clans of these Merry Dancers and that there was a great deal of rivalry between them as to who were the best dancers. Then, in true Romeo and Juliet style, a Nimble Man from one clan fell in love with a Merry Maiden from the other clan. At the Midwinter ball held by The Cailleach – the Queen of Winter – things came to a head and a fight broke out between the clans and so the lights are caused not only by their dancing, but also by the flashes from their clashing swords.

The lights were also well known further south, which says a lot about modern light pollution. In Suffolk they were the Perry Dancers[85] and another English name was the Burning Spears, again reinforcing the idea that the lights were caused by dancing or warring beings who lived in the sky.

Labradorite is the stone of the modern eco warrior or spiritual warrior – those who challenge the lies, corruption and the harm being done to others and our planet. The spiritual warrior also takes on their own fears and aspires to their own spiritual truth. Labradorite and the mighty Warrior Faeries of the Northern Lights, like the Valkyries and Freyja who chose half the slain warriors in Norse Legend, give us the courage and determination to succeed and win against the wrongs and injustices in the world. Eco and spiritual warriors protect rather than attack, protecting rights, people and places. Sometimes our battles are done with ourselves or our bodies, such as fighting off an illness or getting an illness or condition to a stage where we can manage it and get back control of our lives. Spiritual warriors fearlessly radiate their light into the darkness and shine in the face of evil. Think of Labradorite as a shield of light all around you that protects you, your Aura and your energies. It chases away any and all negative energies from your Aura, filling it instead with light and love in the whole rainbow of colours. Labradorite deflects all darkness and negative energies and stops any energy vampires from getting their hooks into you. It doesn't matter how small or how big your cause or battle, these Faeries and Labradorite will protect and empower you, helping you to find that inner light and inner power and to have the stamina to keep going.

Labradorite is also the stone of the Faerie magician and even the modern scientist who seeks to help rather than harm. Contrary to popular belief, Faeries are not anti-science. Faeries know that magic and science are two languages or approaches dealing with the same things. They have no problem with us understanding science as long as we can still retain our sense of awe and wonder, after all science is pretty amazing! What the Faeries really despise is when science harms animals, people or nature, when science tries to act like God or when science throws morality out of the window. Faeries are also very keen for us to show gratitude for what nature provides, which science often forgets in its haste to take from and synthesise nature.

The majesty of the Northern Lights are wondrous to behold, even if you understand that the lights are formed by charged particles from the solar winds colliding with Earth's magnetic fields and atmosphere at the poles. The result is a dizzying and magical array of shimmering colours that weave and dance their way across the sky, mesmerising the watcher and reminding them of the power and beauty of nature. No wonder they are associated with the Norse Goddess of Magic, Freyja. Knowing the science behind the lights can enhance our sense of wonder rather than destroy it and that's what the Faeries love to see. The same is true of the science behind the flashes of light in Labradorite. What causes the iridescent schiller effect, also known as Labradoresence, is the way that light reflects from the planes within the crystal that are not quite parallel. This reminds us that it can be beautiful, magical and deeply empowering not to conform to the norm all the time and to be our magical, individual and unique selves.

For millennia the lights have been seen as portents and this idea isn't just old wives' tales as the lights can tell us some interesting things. In Shetland if the lights moved quickly or angrily then bad weather was forecast, if they moved slowly and gracefully then it was good weather on the way. Over the years we have learned a great deal from the Aurora about our planet, our atmosphere and our Sun. We have learned about Earth's magnetic field and the incredible power of our Sun, which waxes and wanes through an eleven-year cycle. Labradorite makes an excellent companion stone for students and scientists of all kinds, especially those who better want to understand our cosmos and all who dwell within it such as astrologers, astronomers, biologists, chemists, druids, faerieologists, herbalists, historians, geologists, magicians, metaphysicians, physicians, physicists, psychologists, researchers, sociologists and witches. Labradorite has the light of enlightenment in all forms within it. Enlightenment can refer to the light of knowledge and esoteric wisdom as well as to the light that Aurora as Goddess of the Dawn brings us every morning. We can call on Aurora to bring light, knowledge and inspiration into our lives at any time, though magically this can be most effective at dawn.

Meditating with or wearing Labradorite reconnects to our

innate magical abilities and our cosmic origins, after all, we are all children of the cosmos. As Carl Sagan said, *'The nitrogen in our DNA, the calcium in our teeth, the iron in our blood, the carbon in our apple pies were made in the interiors of collapsing stars. We are made of starstuff.'*[86] Working with Labradorite and the Faeries who watch over or dwell within it increases our psychic abilities, enabling us to better see and comprehend the world around us in all its Technicolour glory, including seeing the magical realms and Faeries that exist in and alongside our own realm. Labradorite literally attunes us to the magic and energy of the cosmos. It encourages us to not just use magic or celebrate magic but to *be* the magic. It increases our intuition and acts like a magical library card granting us access to the ancient and magical wisdom of the universe and the ancients, and can help us discover our true destiny or path in life.

Placed on the bedside table overnight Labradorite promotes dreaming and the assimilation of what we have learned or encountered the day before. Further, it aids in balancing the conscious and subconscious parts of our minds and balancing rationality with imagination. Labradorite and the Northern Lights are a gift to us from the Divine and from the Faeries to bring us light, magic and hope, even in the very darkest of times.

Marbles of Ireland

Other Names: Crystalline Limestone

Chemical Composition: $CaCO_3$, the specific chemical composition varies by location

Element: Connemara Marble is Nature and Wood, Cork Marble is Fire, Ulster Marble is Air and Kilkenny Marble is Earth

Season: Connemara Marble is spring, Cork Marble is summer, Kilkenny Marble is autumn and Ulster Marble is winter

Chakra: Ulster Marble is the Crown Chakra, Connemara Marble is the Heart Chakra, Cork Marble is the Sacral Chakra and Kilkenny is the Base Chakra

Birthstone: Connemara Marble is the National Stone for Ireland. Each of the four marbles is linked to the Four Provinces of Ireland so is a birthstone for those born in that geographical area. Ulster Marble is for those born in Ulster, Connemara Marble is for those born in Connacht, Cork Marble is for those born in Munster and Kilkenny Marble is for those born in Leinster

Other: Marble is the State Stone for Vermont

Faerie Monarchs/Deities: Principally Finvarra and Oonagh as the High King and Queen of the Irish Faeries, but also all other Irish Faerie Monarchs like Áine (esp. Cork Marble), Oenghus, Gráinne, Brighid (esp. Kilkenny and Connemara Marble), Niamh, Ogma, Lir, Danu, Manannán and the Dagda

Faeries: The Sidhe of Ireland and the Leprechauns

From the Land of the Sidhe come four different Marbles in the four traditional Fairy colours. Connemara Marble is green, the colour of the Fairy Mounds that gave the Sidhe their name and a colour that many Fairy beings love to dress in. From Cork comes a red Marble, the colour of Fairy bonnets and the Fairy fly agaric mushroom. Ulster Marble is white and reminiscent of the legends of White Fairy Ladies and the colour of the veil between our world and Faerieland. Kilkenny Marble is black, the colour of the deep dark Earth and the inside of the ancient Fairy Mounds. All of these Marbles are thought to help us to connect more deeply with the wisdom of the Sidhe of Ireland.

Crafted and carved marble is beautiful, but much of its beauty seems to either come from its purity, or from its natural inclusions depending on tastes. It is a reminder that perhaps even perfection is in fact made up from lots of flaws and not quite perfects – an interesting lesson for mankind.

Marble is seen to represent authority, power and success and through the ages has been used to adorn grandiose buildings of power such as palaces like that at Versailles in France, banks and prestigious skyscrapers such as the Empire State Building. It also has deeply spiritual connections and was used for temples and tombs such as the Taj Mahal in India. The Taj Mahal is a great example of one of the most magical aspects of Marble, while its outside is composed of gleaming white Marble, inside the tomb are places where coloured Marbles have been used to add extra energy and beauty. Marble is all about the beauty and power inside, some of it shows on the surface, but the eye of the artist searches deeper and sees the wonder and potential inside too. Classic statues such as the Venus de Milo and Michelangelo's David were brought forth from white Marble by very talented artists who could see their works within the Marble before they even lifted a chisel. We too can choose to see what lies within and look beyond the surface.

Just as statues can be brought forth from stone for the world to see and love, Marble encourage us to come out of our shells and to be discovered for our wonderful selves. Too often we hide away, especially in this world where face-to-face interactions have so often been surpassed by doing things online. Marble supports those who are very shy, introverted, on the autism spectrum or those who – for whatever reason – experience nervousness or communication issues when having to deal with other people. The Irish Marbles encourages friendships with other humans and with the Faerie Races of Ireland, allowing us to discover them and them to discover us.

Marbles are metamorphic rocks, meaning that they've been shaped, moulded and changed over time by pressures, temperatures and weathering. Like Marble we've been bashed about by life; we've faced traumas, horrendous pressures, had to weather storms and had both good and bad things happen to us, so working with Marble can be extremely comforting for us as we reflect back on our lives and the things that have made us who we are and the way we are. Just like Marble we've come out of our formation processes with a few flaws, but we've also come out with strength, power, determination and wisdom. The lines on our faces, like the mottling of Marble, enhance our beauty, not detract from it, despite what shallow advertisements may tell you, because those who work with Marble know better, we go deeper than the superficial surface and we acknowledge that we earned those lines like badges or medals of honour.

Believed to lessen perfectionism and criticalness, be it of the self or others, Marble instead encourages original thinking, a healthy questioning outlook and encourages us to take charge of our own lives. We may have had no power over many of the processes and events that formed us, but we can take back our power and take charge moving forward. With its very cleansing energy, Marble has traditional been used to cleanse the blood, urinary, digestive and lymphatic systems, but it also helps us to cleanse ourselves of negative behaviours, negative traits and addictions.

Each of the Irish Marbles is associated with one of the Four Provinces of Ireland and one of the Four Ancient Faerie Cities[87]. As well as the above each Marble has additional metaphysical properties and associations.

Ulster Marble is linked with the Faerie City of Falias, located in the North, and from which the Tuatha Dé Danann brought the Lia Fáil – The Stone of Destiny. Ulster Marble seeks to connect us to our own destiny, to help us find our path in life. It is a deeply spiritual form of Marble, encouraging clarity of mind and spirit. It opens our Crown Chakra and our spiritual and psychic abilities. A stone of sight, it has been used to treat eye problems, sharpen vision, bring on visions and help us to 'see' in terms of sixth sight and extra-sensory perception. Ulster Marble is associated with the Province of Ulster, which has experienced more than its fair share of deep trauma, yet Ulster Marble encourages peace and understanding on a soulful level and always encourage us to look forward optimistically. With its bone-like colour it has traditionally been used for healing broken bones, easing bone aches, toothache and arthritis. It is associated with the Faerie hero Fionn mac Cumhaill.

Kilkenny Marble is linked with the Faerie City of Gorias in the East from whence the Sword of Nuada was brought. Once the sword was drawn from its sheath it was said that no one could escape from it or resist it. In the same way, our Karma is also inescapable. Black Kilkenny Marble shows us the state of our Karma, both from this lifetime and previous ones, and shows us how to improve it. It encourages deep and serious self-reflection and consideration of what we have been through in life and what effect we have had on the lives of others. It is a stone of protection and calm. It was traditionally used to draw off aches and pains. Kilkenny was once known as 'The Marble City' as slabs of Kilkenny Marble were used to line the city streets and in the construction of several local buildings. When it rained the streets famously glistened like dark mirrors. It is the Marble of death and of restful, deep sleep, so very handy for insomniacs. With its sombre energy it has also been used for headstones and tombs, such as the headstone of the Irish political leader Daniel

O'Connell and for the plinth of Richard III's tomb in Leicester Cathedral. As a dark stone it is often linked with Dark Faerie Monarchs such as The Morríghan, and the Monarchs who rule over the dark half of the year like Gráinne and The Cailleach.

Cork Marble symbolises the fiery spear of the Sun God and Faerie King Lugh, which the Tuatha Dé Danann brought with them from the City of Finias in the South. Legends say that no battle was ever sustained this magical spear. Unlike the Sword of Nuada, this spear seems to have been considered a defensive rather than offensive weapon. The red Marble of Cork suggests that we look to our own energies and power and how we use and manage them. Do we use our power protectively or offensively? Do we take care of our own energy systems? Are we getting enough sleep? Do we feel alive or are we permanently exhausted? How can we better take care of our energies and the energies around us? This magical red Marble inspires us with its energy and dynamism, but only if we allow such energies into our lives and can handle it in a positive way. It tempers the aggression and the more dangerous aspects of fire that are often linked with the colour red with the deep wisdom of its Earthy origins. Cork Marble is linked with the Irish Faerie Monarchs of Light, Fire, the Sun and the light half of the year like Lugh, Áine and Brighid. Also the stone of the Irish Goddess of Love and Queen of the Banshees, Clíodhna. **Connemara Marble** with its gorgeous green hues is probably the best known of all the Irish Marbles and has been used as a Birthstone for the whole of Ireland, for Ireland is known as 'The Emerald Isle'. Green is the colour of abundance, growth and verdant nature so it is no wonder that this green Marble is associated with the Faerie treasure from the Western Faerie City of Murias, the Cauldron of the Dagda from which no one ever went unsatisfied. Connemara loves to help us grow and develop, as well as helping to keep our hearts and energy systems healthy for green is also a colour of healing. It has a very upbeat energy and loves to show us how far we have come in life and on our spiritual path, giving us some sense of satisfaction and achievement, but also sharing its optimism with us as we continue on our path for its message to us is, 'Look how far you've come. OK, so you still have a way to go, but hey, you can so do this!' It is a stone of friendship, linked with the concept of the *Anam Cara* – 'Soul Friend' – as pieces and presents of Connemara Marble have long been gifted as tokens of friendship and peace. It also encourages us to forge new friendships and to be our own friend. Like Aventurine, Connemara Marble helps plants thrive. Often it is associated with Brighid because she was said to have worn a mantle or cloak of the same green as Connemara Marble. Another association is with the Faerie Gods and Goddesses of the Wild Wood such as The Dagda and Flidais. Connemara Marble is a particular favourite of Leprechauns.

Moonstone

Other Names: Hecatolite, Chandra Kanta Moni (Hindi for 'Wife of the Moon'), the Dream Stone or Feldspar
Chemical Composition: $KAlSi_3O_8$
Element: Spirit, Magic and Cosmos
Season: Winter
Planet: The Moon
Chakra: Third Eye and Crown
Birthstone: June
Other: Day stone for Mondays, State Gemstone of Florida
Faerie Monarchs/Deities: Arianrhod, Selene, Diana, Gwydion, Mani, Thoth, Lona, Changxi, Sin, Mahina, Awilix and all the Moon Gods and Goddesses around the world
Faeries: All Faeries who love to dance beneath the Full Moon, especially the Lunantishee, plus the Mermaids and Morgens

Moonstone comes in several colours including white, peach and grey, all with a milky sheen and a luminous opalescence. Here Moonstone shows us our own inner light and inner soul. Like Labradorite, which also shares the same schiller effect, Moonstone is thought to be a very lucky and magical stone. The Romans thought it was solidified moonlight and there are many references to the Moon being a jewel or gemstone glittering in the sky.

Hail to thee, thou new moon,
Guiding jewel of gentleness!
I am bending my knee to thee,
I am offering thee my love.[88]

Sometimes, when the light is right, Moonstone can appear to glow as if it is emitting its own light. Legends say that its glow and energies wax and wane with the phases of the Moon, just like the 'Moonstone' (which was technically a Diamond) in the 19th century Gothic novel of the same name by Wilkie Collins.

Faeries of all kinds adore Moonstone because it contains the power and energy of the Full Moon, which they love to celebrate, for it is beneath the Full Moon that Faeries love to dance and hold their revels. There are many ancient sites and stones that Faeries are said to dance around on the night of the Full Moon, such as around the King of the Faeries Chair, which is in fact a set of Roman ruins near Kenchester[89], around the Queen of the Faeries Chair – a rock formation on the Yorkshire Border[90] – and around the three concentric stone circles of the Avebury complex in Wiltshire[91]. Many Faerie encounters are also reported as occurring at the time of the Full Moon such as the Faeries knocking on Mari Siôn's door in Llanddeusant[92] and for centuries local lore has spoken of a Faerie Knight emerging from Wandlebury Hill Fort on the night of the Full Moon[93]. Mermaids and Morgens also adore Moonstone and they are deeply affected by the Moon because they dwell in the tidal oceans. It is thought that Faeries and Mermaids are easier to see and sense by the light of the Moon, so Moonstone has often been credited with allowing people to see and communicate with Faeries and Mermaids.

Just as the Moon affects the tides, many believe that humans are also influenced by the cycles of the Moon in all sorts of ways. There are many people around the world, especially by coasts, who still depend on knowing and working around the tide times. There are still places where tides can cut communities off, even in the UK, such as at Mersea Island with its often-flooded causeway. Like Aquamarine, Moonstone was often carried as a talisman for safe travel, especially across water, and for favourable tides and winds.

The idea that humans are affected by the Moon's cycles is really not that far out, after all we are 60 percent water and studies have shown that many women's cycles tally with that of the Moon. Moonstone has long been used to help women balance their hormones and regulate their monthly cycles, but it is reputed to balance all liquids in the human body, such as the lymphatic and urinary systems as well as our hormonal ones. Furthermore, Moonstone is said to help balance our emotions, which can certainly feel water based when they wash over us like waves, and our biorhythms. Moonstone soothes the stresses and tensions that we have about or as a result of our cycles in life and soothes any dis-ease that arises from them. Many people, including myself, report that their sleep cycles are affected by the Moon, with people saying that they either sleep much better or much worse at the time of the Full Moon. It's also common for people to manage their hair and nails by the Moon, as if we cut them during the waxing stage, it is thought to promote their growth, and if we cut them during the waning Moon, they allegedly grow more slowly. Elixirs of Moonstone have long been used for beautification and to soothe and heal skin and hair problems. There's also an old wives' tale that our mental health and mental and chemical cycles are affected by the Moon. It is where we get the term *lunatic* from, deriving from *lunaticus* meaning something like 'moonstruck'.

The Lunantishee are closely associated with Moonstone as their name of 'Moon-Sidhe' or 'Moon-Faeries' suggests. These are the fiercely protective Faerie Guardians of the blackthorn[94] who highlight to us the need for us to protect ourselves, our homes and our personal energies. Generally these Faeries are known to be antagonistic to humans, which is no surprise when you consider how mankind has destroyed most of the ancient hedgerows that provided homes for the Faeries and for wildlife. Yet, like the thorns of the blackthorn itself, their spiky nature is protective, not offensive, as they are merely looking to protect themselves. If you are willing to demonstrate to them that you are serious about working with them and working towards the conservation of their habitat, they may be prepared to share with you some of their incredible magical skills or sense of mystery.

The Lunantishee, like many Faeries and our ancestors, worship the Moon Goddess. There are literally hundreds of Moon Goddesses found all over the world: Arianrhod from Wales whose name means 'Silver Wheel', the Roman Goddesses Luna and Diana, whose bow was thought to depict the crescent Moon, the Greek Selene, the Aztec Mama Killa, the Finnish Kuu, whose name is still used as the Finnish word for the Moon, the Chinese Changxi and the Polynesian Mahina are just a few examples. Although in modern Faerie Witchcraft, Druidry and Wicca, the Moon is often seen as female, in times past it wasn't that simple. There are many Moon Gods from around the world, all of whom, like the Goddesses, are linked to Moonstone, such as Thoth from Ancient Egypt, Mani from Norse Mythology, Hermes from Ancient Greece, Sin from Ancient Mesopotamia, Coniraya from Incan Mythology and Tsukiyomi from Japan. Even the Man in the Moon can be seen as a half-lost memory of the Moon God. Sometimes the Moon Deity is seen as both God and Goddess such as the Aztec Metztli, Awilix of K'iche' Maya Mythology and Mano/Manna of Saami Mythology. If you wish to work with any Moon Deity or Moon-loving Faerie, Moonstone can be a very useful conduit and spiritual companion, but it will ask you to work with the phases of the Moon in your magical workings and to acknowledge the effect the Moon has on your mundane as well as magical life.

Moonstone is often used to help us to get in touch with our feminine intuition and our feminine sides, but it can also help us to get in contact with our male sides too and to balance them both beautifully and gracefully. Moonstone really is a stone of balance, helping us to explore and balance our emotions. It supports us lovingly in working through our phobias, fears and emotional issues, washing away emotional blockages and releasing repressed emotions. If you feel emotionally stuck in any way, work with Moonstone and Aquamarine to gently clear any blockages. It reveals emotional truths and increases emotional intelligence. Moonstone shows us all our insecurities and anxieties, shining a soft, gentle light on their true origins so that we might seek and deal with their real and deep causes. Moonstone can get us out of our heads and cerebral way of thinking, connecting us with our heart and emotional desires. Moonstone's message is to feel rather than think and to trust our divinely given intuition.

Moonstone is an ideal companion for those who live life from a place of love, for those learning emotional lessons, and for those who live, think and feel outside the box, for it loves to work with the eclectic or eccentric soul who sees the world differently. Just as things appear different in moonlight from how they do in sunlight, Moonstone shows us how to see things differently and in entirely new and revolutionary ways. It literally opens our minds to the wonder of the universe as it opens our Crown Chakra. In particular it enables us to see things from the perspectives of others and from a more emotional point of view. Differences are beautiful and they can be incredibly enlightening. Why should we all be the same? Wouldn't that be boring? Moonstone encourages our individuality and guides us to be our extraordinary and stunning selves.

Moonstone assists us with new beginnings and new starts because it helps us to move towards the light while learning from the darkness and events that have happened. Like the Moon, emotions, situations, circumstances and events come and go or wax and wane. Moonstone is also ideal for those whose new starts include puberty and becoming an adult, pregnancy or motherhood/fatherhood, for those moving on from parent to the king or queen phase once the children have left the nest, or from moving from adult to king and queen once we become a respected elder.

Bringing us vivid dreams, psychic dreams, sweet dreams, better dream recall and encouraging lucid dreaming, Moonstone is also called 'the Dream Stone'. It also demonstrates our need to get a good night's sleep, to daydream and to fantasise to help keep our minds healthy.

Moonstone has long been credited with mystical and magical powers, and working with Moonstone enhances our magical workings, our charms and enchantments. It has also been revered for centuries, especially in India, as a holy stone. If you are feeling lost, distracted or a little Pixy-led, Moonstone reminds us that life is about the journey, not the destination and cheekily points out that when we work with Faeries being a little Pixy-led is inevitable, so we may as well enjoy it. After all, in being Pixy-led we are being guided by the Fae to things and places that we may not otherwise have encountered. You could find that by becoming a little lost or enchanted you end up exactly where you are meant to be and you can bet they've done it for a good reason, even if they don't chose to share that reason with you at the time.

Moonstone loves to be cleansed and charged beneath the light of the Full Moon. It will always encourage Faeries to come out and play.

Moss and Tree Agate

Chemical Composition: SiO_2 The green inclusions are Hornblende $(Ca_2(Mg, Fe, Al)_5 (Al, Si)_8 O_{22}(OH)_2)$ or Chlorite (ClO_2) and when these are oxidised can give the inclusions a red tint

Element: Earth, Wood, Nature and Spirit

Season: Summer

Planet: Earth

Chakra: Heart and Earth Star

Birthstone: May, June and Gemini

Faerie Monarchs/Deities: The Green Man/Viridios, Herne/ Cernunnos, Karnuntina, Nemetona, Flidais, Medeina, Arduinna and Tapi and Mielikki, Tāne-mahuta, Medziojna and all the many deities associated with woods and forests

Faeries: Satyrs, Hamadryads and Dryads, Forest Elves, the Oakmen, Meliae, Skogsrå, Huldra, Niägriusar and Ngen

Moss Agate is a form of clear-ish Quartz with green inclusions. Tree Agate has the same inclusions, but against a whiter or more opaque form of Quartz. Both of these are very much stones of nature. While light green Aventurine has a softer, more gentle energy and represents plants, shrubs and some of the more graceful trees, Moss and Tree Agate have a deeper, darker and far wilder energy and represent the wilderness and wild ancient forests. They owe their names to the dendritic or moss-like effect of the green inclusions; they do not actually include any organic matter, unlike Jet and Amber.

Sadly there are few if any really wild and natural places left on this planet, even what we think of today as untouched is in fact managed. The word forest that we now apply to large wooded areas originally meant 'reserve' and many of Britain's forests have probably only survived because they were once royal reserves and hunting grounds. Millennia ago the land masses were covered by vast thick forests. All that's left today are fragments. The largest of these is the Taiga or the Great Boreal Forest, which spreads across the northern parts of Scandinavia, Russia, Kazakhstan, Mongolia and Japan. Across the Pacific it also spreads across inland Alaska and Canada, where it is known as the Northwoods. Even today it is so vast large that it is the largest biome on Earth, apart from the oceans. This ancient and vast forest is deeply linked to the powerful, ancient and wild energies of Moss and Tree Agate as are the other forests that remain, such as Epping Forest in Essex, Sherwood Forest in Nottinghamshire and the Black Forest of Germany. Yet Mother Nature has the power to reclaim what mankind takes from her, if, or rather when, she gets the chance. Weeds and saplings grow from cracks in our urban pavements in a very real physical and more metaphysical and spiritual sense, and areas that humans abandon are soon swamped by shrubs.

Deforestation on an epic scale is sadly nothing new for Neolithic man cleared vast swathes of forest for land for his animals to graze, then the likes of the British Navy felled entire forests to build wooden war ships. Today we still continue mercilessly to destroy our woodlands and forests. However, there is another way. The Faeries wish us to learn from the past, our past mistakes and our mismanagement of nature. They tell us not to support deforestation, but to instead support projects that reforest and re-wild. They desperately want us to learn to take better care of ourselves, each other and the planet. The Faeries also ask us to recycle paper, to buy recycled paper and to buy products with the seal of the Forest Stewardship Council and other similar schemes that promote responsible forest management and replace any trees felled, sometimes several times over.

Faeries encourage us to plant more trees, not just in our own gardens and parks, but also out in the forests and there are schemes where you can sponsor just a tree if you have no space in which you can plant one of your own. These trees provide Faeries and wildlife with much-needed refuge and food. If possible it is much nicer if you can see or visit your tree(s) on a regular or semi-regular basis so that you can enjoy seeing it grow and get to know the Dryad that lives within it. In Scandinavia and Germany there has long been the lovely tradition of the *Tuntre* – 'Farm Tree', which not only represented the World Tree, but also provided a home for local Nature Spirits, invoking their kindness and help around the place. After all, better that they have somewhere nice to live rather than them making mischief around the farm. The trees and their residents offered the farm protection, which is why they were also sometimes called *Vårdträd* – 'Warden Trees'. The Farm Tree is an idea that it is lovely to try, and it is very special to see the trees grow over the years that you live in a specific house. It is also great to plant a tree when you have a child and to watch both tree and child grow over the years. These Farm Trees may have been around for centuries and others may be newer, perhaps planted by new owners who wish to make friends with the local Faeries. To fell one of these trees was considered a very serious offence that would invoke the wrath of the Faerie who occupied it. Regular offerings were made to the trees and the Faeries. There were even specific races of Faeries who were said to live in these Farm Trees such as the Brownie-like Niägriusar of the Faroe Islands.

Forests feature heavily in our Faerie tales where they are often seen to be alive or a character in their own right. They are dark, foreboding, terrifying places inhabited by wolves, bears, Witches and supernatural monsters, where heroes and heroines are easily lost and must face many challenges. These forests represent our darker sides, our subconscious and our shadow selves. After all the real monsters in the forest are the human beings who mercilessly chop them down and who try to 'civilise' the wild. Moss and Tree Agate challenge us to look at our own true selves for we are humans and humans are mammals like the wolves and bears. We evolved from primates who lived in the forests, so really the forests are our ancient homes, as indeed was water if you go back even further in our evolutionary history. Moss and Tree Agate take us safely into and through our own inner wild woods so we can safely explore and discover our subconscious and shadow selves through dreams and meditation.

Every year there are said to be great battles in the woods or great metamorphoses depending on the legend. Every Midsummer and Midwinter the Holly King of the evergreens does battle with the Oak King of the deciduous trees[95]. At Midsummer the Dark Holly King wins and rules over the dark half of the year, while the Oak King wins at Midwinter and so rules the light half of the year – this is akin to the battling between the Faerie Kings Gwynn ap Nudd and Gwythyr ap Greidawl over Creiddylad or Guinevere. Moss Agate, with its darker aspect, does seem to represent the energies of the Holly King and the lighter tones of Tree Agate relate to the Oak King. There is a similar concept – without the violence – with hawthorn and blackthorn. The hawthorn, the light sister, rules over the summer and her reign starts with the blossoming of the may and runs until Samhain, while the blackthorn, the dark sister, rules from Samhain when her berries ripen through until Beltane. Both Moss and Tree Agate are great companions through times of change and growth. They help us to tune in to the changing energies of the natural world around us as the seasons turn.

Moss and Tree Agate connect us to the mysteries of the Great World Tree of Life, known by many names and to many cultures all over the world. The type of tree naturally varies with location and has been the ash, the yew, the apple, the sycamore, the bodhi and others. This life-giving tree connects the Upper Realms of the Gods, the Middle Realm of man and the Lower Realm of the Dwarfs and the dead. Like us this tree gets its nourishment from the Earth, but also reaches to the Heavens with its branches. In many creation myths, the first people were created from trees. In Norse Legend the first man was made from an ash tree while the first woman was made from the elm or the rowan[96]. In Persian mythology, Mashya and Mashyana were two trees who became the first man and the first woman[97].

We are intrinsically drawn to woods and forests, perhaps because on some level we recognise them as a home from home, and walking in woodlands is known to have calming effects and be good for our physical and psychological health[98]. Working with Moss and Tree Agate also links us to the energies of the green woods and forests, which can benefit our sense of wellbeing and health, and, with the assistance of these deep green Agates, we can journey in dreams and meditations to ancient forests and woodlands, which is especially useful if for any reason we can't do the real thing.

We think that we have mastered our own wild nature, but have we really? Moss and Tree Agate encourage us to get in touch with our wild inner self as a source of our power and strength. This doesn't mean that we should go wild, rather that we should acknowledge what we really are and know that we are one with nature and the other animals and beings that we share this planet with. Moss and Tree Agate show us how strong and resilient we are and how much we have been through and how much we have grown. After all, like the acorn grows to the sapling and then on to the mighty oak, so too do we grow in life. We also recognise our innate connection to and love of trees and their Faeries through our names. So many of us have names that derive from trees, like Ackley (from oak), Ashton, Atwood, Birch, Hayley (ley referring to a wood or clearing therein), Holt, Hurst, Lendelius (from the lime), Rowan, Sawyer (as in woodworker), Sylvia ('Lady of the Wood'), Willow, Woodley, Yves (from yew), etc.

Forests have many guardians who watch over the trees, the animals and the forest as a whole being or biome. These guardians exist all over the world and are known by many names. In Sweden there are the Skogsrå ('Forest Guardian')[99] and the Ulldra/Huldra who was beautiful from the front, but hollow like a log from behind[100], in Germany there were the Wood Wives, in Ancient Greece there were the Dryads of the trees, the Hamadryads of the oak, the Meliae of the ash trees and the goat-like Satyrs, from England come the Dwarfish Oakmen who protect oak trees and in the South Americas there are the Nge̲n-mawida watching over the trees. There are also countless Faerie Monarchs and Deities who watch over or are associated with the wild woods, including the Celtic Herne/Cernunnos, the Gaulish Karnuntina, the Greek Pan, the Irish Flidais, the Roman Viridios, the Finnish Mielikki and Tapio, the Lithuanian Medeina, the Egyptian Ash, the Māori Tāne, and the Gaulish Arduinna who gave her name to the Ardennes Forest. If you wish to connect with any of these Faerie Beings or Monarchs, Moss and Tree Agate can be valuable go-betweens and will help you connect to their energies and wisdom.

Moss and Tree Agates contain the wisdom and magic of the ancient forests. After all in Faerie Tales many forests are enchanted or bewitched. In the Germanic and Celtic languages there are several words related to wisdom that derive from the root word of *vid/wit* and wydd respectively, both meaning 'wood'. These include *witiga* ('wisdom'), *witan* ('wise men' and the name of the assembly who counselled the King in Anglo-Saxon England). We can still find its influence in modern English in the words dr*uid*, *wit*ch or *wiz*ard.

Carry or wear Moss or Tree Agate if you wish to strengthen your links to the tree kingdom and the many types of Tree Faeries. These stones are beloved by horticulturalists, gardeners, forest bathers and herbalists. Placed in the garden or around trees they will support and nurture the tree and its Faeries, just as they can do for us if placed in the home or kept on our person. With their deep green hues, these are stone of powerful healing that are reputed to restore and rejuvenate us right down to the ancestral and DNA levels. Like the sap circulation systems of trees, we have our circulatory systems and these Agates have long been thought to cleanse our circulatory, endocrine and lymphatic systems, boosting our immune systems and promoting wellbeing.

Moss and Tree Agates are the stones of the environmentalist and Earth-healer for they heal the Earth and our connection to her, which can become damaged or withered by our living in the concrete jungle. They epitomise the energy of the modern Green movement and support us in making changes so that we can live a greener and healthier lifestyle.

Moss and Tree Agate highlight our need to get out and about into nature, to take strolls through parks or local woods. They enable us to communicate with trees and their Faeries, building up strong relationships and great rapport over time. Being deep green stones, they help us to communicate with other beings on the level of the Heart Chakra and through our Earth Star where we connect to Mother Earth below us, just as trees do with their roots.

Preseli Bluestone

Other Names: Stonehenge Stone, the Shaman's Stone, Britain's Birthstone or Spotted/Unspotted Dolerite

Chemical Composition: Plagioclase Feldspar (Calcium Feldspar – $CaAlSi3O8$) and Augite $(Ca,Na)(Mg,Fe,Al,Ti)(Si,Al)_2O_6$. There are often traces of other minerals such as Iron (Fe) and Copper Pyrites $(CuFeS_2)$

Element: Water, Deep Earth and Cosmos

Season: Winter/summer especially at the times of the solstices

Planet: The entire night sky, with all the wondrous sparkling stars

Chakra: Sacral and Earth Star

Birthstone: Birthstone for all those born in Britain, especially those born in Wales

Other: National Stone of Wales

Faerie Monarchs/Deities: All Welsh Faerie Monarchs such as Ceridwen, Branwen, Brân the Blessed, Gwynn ap Nudd, Don, Arianrhod, Olwen, Llew, Manawydan and Gwydion. Also Merlin, Uther Pendragon, Ambrosius and King Arthur

Faeries: All Welsh Faeries such as the Morgens, the Tylwyth Teg, the Bwbach, the Ellyllon and the Gwragedd Annwn. Also Giants

Our ancestors considered this stone so special and so magical that blocks of it were taken more than 150 miles, or 230km, from the Preseli Hills of Wales to Salisbury Plain in Somerset in order to construct a stone circle. If you ever get the chance to handle Preseli Bluestone you will find that not only it is surprisingly warm to the touch for a stone, it is also pretty heavy for its size, so transporting it over that huge distance was no mean feat. Due to this Bluestone shows us how to be creative and ingenious in overcoming obstacles and staying the course when things get tough.

Those same Welsh Bluestones can still be seen today as Stonehenge's centre arrangement. Stonehenge has a timeless quality, but the monument was not always as it looks today; in fact it has been changed and rearranged many times over the millennia. It began life about 5,000 years ago as a circular bank and ditch enclosure of chalk. In time wooden posts were added to mark the Sun and Moon rises and then a full timber circle. Archaeologists believe it was about 2600 BC when the Bluestones were brought from Wales to form a circle of stones. The giant Sarsens that form the infamous trilithons were brought to the site later and the Bluestones then rearranged within them. It is not known for certain whether or not the Bluestone circle had already existed elsewhere first. The Arthurian legends tell us that it did and potentially this is a half-forgotten folk memory, though of course it could just be a good yarn. In his 12th Century work, *Historia Regum Britanniae* ('History of the Kings of Britain'), Geoffrey of Monmouth tells us that Stonehenge was originally built by Giants who dragged the stones from Africa to Mount Killaraus in Ireland because they had magical healing properties. Later Aurelius Ambrosius informed the wizard Merlin that he wished to erect a timeless monument at Salisbury to the thousands of Celts and Romano-Celts who had been slain by the invading Saxons. Merlin suggested that Stonehenge would make an excellent memorial and so thousands of knights were dispatched to Ireland to seize it. Yet despite all their best efforts the knights failed to move any of the stones. After having a bit of a laugh at the knight's efforts, Merlin, using the magic he learned from the Faeries, conjured the stones to Salisbury Plain, where they still stand today.

It is an intriguing story, but seeing as Preseli Bluestone is a stone that encourages us to seek the truth in legends and the lesson in fables we have to ask, is any of it true? Well, yes, some of it probably is. Stonehenge predates the time of Ambrosius and Merlin by millennia (and it also predates the druids with whom it is closely linked) so that part isn't true. Yet the idea that it was built by Giants could well have some truth once you consider that Faeries and Giants are often how we perceive our ancestors, especially those who achieved great feats. We literally 'big them up' in myth and legend until the ancestor or hero/heroine develops magical powers or majestic height. The Irish link is also what makes many think that the tale tells of a folk memory of the journey of the Bluestones for the Preseli area is far away to the west, as is Ireland. Indeed, the Preselis lie on the ancient Ireland/Wessex trade and travel route. It is also possible that folk memory has mixed up Ireland and Preseli because some of the stones were brought over water from Milford Haven to Bristol and up the River Avon. It is also theorised that the idea of Stonehenge as a memorial to the dead is also a folk memory – in time, Ambrosius, Uther Pendragon and Constantine III were all said to have been buried inside the stone circle.

Theories as to the purpose of Stonehenge come and go like fashions. What's trendy with archaeologists one decade is ridiculed in the next before becoming popular yet again later on. One of the current theories is that Stonehenge was a place of healing and that the Bluestones were credited with healing and magical powers just as Merlin said. Monmouth's tale says that whenever the Giant's fell ill they would take baths at the base of the stones, making sure that the water was run over the stones to absorb some of their healing power first[101]. Herbs were also added to such water imbued by Bluestones to make healing potions and remedies. In Wales where the Bluestones originate they are also linked with healing and water in exactly the same way. Bluestone is a favourite of the Welsh Water Faeries, the *Gwragedd Annwn*, who are renowned for their magical healing skills, which they taught to mankind. In working with water, Bluestone and these kindly Faeries we can discover the many benefits of water for our wellbeing.

Stonehenge has been known by many names in its history, most of which have been long forgotten. Its current name derives from the Saxon for 'Hanging Stones' probably referring to the Sarsen lintels. Other names include *Chorea Gigantum* – 'Giant's Dance or Choir', which fits with Monmouth's tale, and *Cor Gawr*[102], which means 'Great Choir'. Here we see Stonehenge as a Giant's Faerie Ring where they dance and have their music. The stone circles of Cornwall are also sometimes referred to as *Dawns-Mên* or 'Stone Dances'[103]. Like many other stone circles, Stonehenge is a giant Faerie portal, even seeing pictures of can take us away to Faerieland because its energy is so strong. Faerie music is renowned to be magical and healing and many old folk tunes have Faerie origins or are Faerie inspired. Some even believe that music itself was a gift from the Faeries because its effects are so magical. In recent times, archaeologists have investigated the musical aspects of Stonehenge and found that the stones create some very strange acoustic effects[104]. Preseli Bluestone does indeed love music and highlights the benefits of music and sound healing for our health and wellbeing. Bluestone encourages you to bring music and movement into your life and it cares not whether you attend grand classical concerts or just have the radio on when driving somewhere, as long as you are engaging with its power. Music is enchanting; it can change our mood, enhance memory and drag up memories that we thought were long forgotten. In this same way Bluestone brings up ancient memories from deep within us and connects us to ancestral memories and wisdom. It has also traditionally been used to aid those with memory issues or impairments and to help actors remember their lines and public speakers to give great speeches.

What we call Preseli Bluestone is a mix of Welsh dolerites, some plain and some spotted. They are not homogenous and with their patterning they are as unique as we are and they encourage us to be unique. The name Bluestone may seem odd to many for it is not really blue at all. It is more of a greyish-green. The confusion is down to the Welsh word *glas,* which is often interpreted as meaning 'blue', but what it really means is 'green-blue-grey'. The spotted form of Preseli Bluestone has inclusions of white material, which may be Quartz or Feldspar. It is often said that these white inclusions look like the stars against the darker hues of the stone's base colours. This is very apt considering Stonehenge's role as a giant astronomical calendar and these star-like inclusions could well be why our ancestors chose to use it. It's worth noting that the *Chorea* or 'Dance' part of *Chorea Gigantum* can just as easily refer to the movement or circling of the planets and stars as it does to a round dance and Stonehenge has long been used to mark astronomical events and celestial movements. This is why this stone is linked with the Faerie Monarchs of the celestial bodies such as Arianrhod, the Welsh Moon Goddess whose name means 'Silver Wheel', and may refer to the circle of the Full Moon or the path of the circling silver stars. Preseli Bluestone certainly has a celestial vibe to it, for it is a deeply spiritual and magical stone that opens us to the realms of the heavens, the Earth beneath our feet and to the realm of Faeries and our ancestors. Earth-healers, astronomers, astrologers and archaeologists are all intrinsically drawn to this stone. Bluestone opens our Chakras for healing and, with its circular arrangement of stones, Stonehenge is like a giant Chakra. Some even claim Stonehenge is the Sacral Chakra or the oomphalos/navel of the planet. Working with Bluestone educates us about our energy systems and the energy systems of the Earth for it is inherently connected to them.

Much is made of the fact that Bluestone is the Stonehenge Stone, but it has also been used to build several other special and sacred monuments back in Wales with Faerie connections. Its energies connect us to all of these sacred sites and others all around the world, for they are all connected by invisible energy lines. The area around the Preseli Hills, from where Preseli Bluestone comes from and is named after, is a land steeped in Faerie and Celtic legends; the area was once called *Gwlad Hud a Lledrith* or 'The Land of Myth and Enchantment'. It was, and still is, a little bit of Faerieland in our realm and reputedly even has its own mystical veil separating it from the rest of the world[105]. Below Carn Menyn, where some of the Stonehenge stones were quarried, lies Gors Fawr Stone Circle, which is made up of various Dolerites including some of Preseli Bluestone. Local legends say that if you find the exact centre of the circle (which is a challenge because it is actually egg-shaped) and jump up and down three times a portal will open beneath you and you will fall into Faerieland, rather like Alice down the rabbit hole. The legends do not, however, mention how to get back. The impressive Waun Mawn Standing Stone, which stands in a small pool of water, is also of Bluestone. Such pools of water are home to the Morgens and Gwragedd Annwn and are traditionally considered portals into the Faerie Otherworld, which is one of the reasons so many votive objects were cast into bodies of water. Another Welsh Bluestone monument is the Pentre Ifan Dolmen, which was a legendary place of druidic initiation and a Faerie Haunt[106]. The Fair Folk spied at Pentre Ifan were of the Welsh Faerie Race known as the *Tylwyth Teg* – 'The Fair Family' who never grow old, can fly about at will and have been known to assist folk with divination. Preseli Bluestone is a very Faerie stone that opens channels of communication with all Faeries, especially those from Wales or with a Welsh link such as Morgan le Fay and Ceridwen, and Pentre Ifan is also known as Ceridwen's Cauldron. It allows Faerie wisdom and magic to flow into our lives in countless ways. Those who practise divination may like to keep a Bluestone with their tools or to use a pendulum or wand of Bluestone, which is especially potent for any Earth-healing or ancestral-healing work.

Preseli Bluestone is very powerful and dramatic. It loves the kind of drama and ritual that was played out at Stonehenge in times past and is still played out today. It loves myths, legends, Faerie tales and folklore, no wonder it features so heavily in them. Bluestone encourages us to look at the drama and rituals in our lives and to remember the old stories that we have heard and passed on in order to keep them alive. You will have heard or read old stories and legends as a child and maybe told them to your own children. Your family may have little rituals that it performs at certain times of year or to mark certain life events and there may be old rituals that are still practised in your area such as the Helston Furry Dance, Up Helly Aa in the Shetlands, or the bonfires of Bonfire Night or St John's Eve. Preseli Bluestone urges us to acknowledge the importance of rituals and through them to connect to the ancestors who went before us and the generations yet to come – this epitomises the true timelessness of this stone. It teaches us to look at the power of drama, of theatre and even of modern TV, and of how we ourselves act with others for as Shakespeare wrote in *As You Like It*:

All the world's a stage,
And all the men and women merely players;
They have their exits and their entrances,
And one man in his time plays many parts...[107]

Drama therapy, like sound therapy, can have powerful and very positive effects on us. Drama, like music, also brings us together just as the great rituals at sacred sites would have done.

Preseli Bluestone is a strangely social stone, perhaps that's why so many are brought together to create stone circles and dolmens. Just as the ancient rituals observed at Stonehenge would have brought communities together to mark the Solstices, Bluestone encourages us to come together to celebrate. It reveals us that we are not alone, that there are other Faerie workers out there who we can work with, learn from, hold rituals with and simply socialise with. It also shows us our own communities where we love and the roles we can play within those. We are also reminded that when working with Faeries we can become a part of their community too. Importantly Preseli Bluestone and its Faeries wish us to come together to protect sacred sites and to protect each other from injustices and oppression of any form.

Creating a grid or Faerie Circle with Preseli Bluestone is incredibly empowering. It is like having your own Stonehenge or Gors Fawr to work with and opens a sacred and protected space for the Faeries to gather in and for you to work in. A little goes a long way with this powerful stone, so even small tumblestones work very nicely. If you feel drawn to Ancient Britain or Wales and to the stories, deities and Faeries of those lands, Preseli Bluestone will assist you in connecting to them on a deeper level.

Preseli Bluestone is the stone of the shaman, especially the Faerie shaman as it acts as an initiation stone, through which the Faeries initiate us into their ways. It links us to ancient wisdom and ancient natural magic of the deep Earth and the high heavens. Through us it connects the Earth with the cosmos, blending their vibrations and magic. The spotted version, with its light and dark colour combination, balances our different energies and aspects, the yin/yang, the male/female, the conscious/unconscious mind, and the heart/head in a gentle, but effective manner. Bluestone can calm us or energise us, depending on what we need at the time.

Rose Quartz

Other Names: Pink Quartz, Bohemian Ruby, the Stone of Love or the Stone of Romance

Chemical Composition: SiO_2 The pink colour is from trace amounts of Titanium (Ti), Iron (Fe) or Manganese (Mn)

Element: Air

Season: Early summer, around the time of Beltane

Planet: Venus

Chakra: Heart

Birthstone: January, Cancer and Taurus

Faerie Monarchs/Deities: All deities associated with love, for example, Branwen, Oenghus, Rhiannon, Clíodhna, Hathor, Freyja, Frigg, Lofn, Živa, Prende, Kwan Yin, Venus and Aphrodite

Faeries: All linked with love in any form, plus the Flower Faeries

Rose Quartz has the most beautiful soft pink hues that cannot help but calm and soothe you as soon as you cast your eyes upon it. It is an incredibly gentle stone with a very soft, loving energy that feels like a squishy security blanket into which you can sink and let all your cares and worries float away.

It is *the* stone of love and teaches us not to judge when it comes to love. Love is blind, it is unpredictable, intense and sometimes overwhelming. Love happens or it doesn't, although sometimes it takes many years to bloom. Despite what Faerie tales, romantic comedies and romance novels might say, there's no magic formula or magic spell that can make love happen if it's not there. Love can be reciprocated or can be one way. We say that we love all sorts of things from other people to inanimate objects, but do we really mean it? Love can be physical, mental or spiritual or all three. It can be passive and gentle or it can be fierce and passionate. Modern scientists argue that love is little more than a chemical reaction in our brain, but the ancients viewed it as being felt from the heart because they knew how central love and the heart are to us as human beings.

The stone of unconditional love; Rose Quartz opens the heart to love in all its forms. It wishes us to feel love and be loved. This loving stone encourages us to love deeply, to love others and love ourselves. It shows us that we are just as deserving of love as anyone else and helps us to overcome any fears or blockages about love that we may have. It can aid those with low self-esteem or low self-worth. Roes Quartz and its Faeries show us the way to inner happiness that is born from love and compassion. Helping us to sympathise and empathise with others, it connects us all through love and through our Heart Chakras, which are at the very centre of our bodies and our beings.

Rose Quartz is the stone of romance, with the soft hues of candlelit dinners, the pink squishiness of a hug and the warm pink tones of that fuzzy feeling that we get when we're in love. Rose Quartz keeps love alive and is the very essence and vibration of love. Rose Quartz is also the colour of pink rose petals, hence its name. While nowadays red roses are usually the flower of love and passion, pink flowers also represent love of the more romantic kind. In the Victorian language of flowers, which used flowers to convey messages, pink roses represented romantic love[108], happiness and thankfulness. Other similarly coloured pink flowers also had meanings: pink carnations speak of sweet memories of love, pink dianthus symbolises affection, pink orchids and pink tulips are tokens of love, pink heather represents luck in love and peonies symbolise happy marriage, as indeed they do in Chinese culture and Feng Shui. Pink peonies are often considered the King or Gentleman of Flowers[109] while pink roses are the Queen or Lady of Flowers.

Rose Quartz is adored by all the Flower Faeries, not just those who watch over and care for pink blooms. Keeping Rose Quartz by flowers will enhance their blooms and show the Flower Faeries that you're thinking of them and sending love their way. Just as the Flower Faeries enable the flowers that they tend to grow in love, they can help us to grow in love too. Rose Quartz represents the Faeries' deep love and reverence for nature and Mother Earth, and this is something they are very keen to enhance and develop in us. They wish us to learn to really love and care for Mother Earth and to see how beautiful and loving She is – look at all the beauty, wonder and nourishment that She provides for us, She is a very loving Mother indeed. The Faeries also wish to show us how loved we are by the Divine, by the Star Father, God, Goddess, the Universe or whatever name you choose to use and how to develop a loving relationship with the Divine. Although they may have a funny of way of showing it, the Faeries also wish us to know that they love us as they do all beings. If you're reading this book then I'm guessing that you love Faeries and love stones too!

Rose Quartz helps us to connect with others on the heart level, sometimes without letting our heads get in the way. Many children love Faeries and other beings unconditionally, but are then repeatedly told they are being 'silly' or 'childish' for believing in Faeries, which then hardens their heart and stops that free flow of love. We've all had those times where someone has made some unpleasant comment about someone that we love or how we love, which has then affected our love in some way. We may have even been told that our love is disapproved of because our lover is of another race, nationality, has a child with another, or is of the same gender as us. Really that's the problem of the disapproving, narrow-minded person who made those nasty comments, it's not your problem at all, so don't let it become your problem! Some of us have been forced to choose between the parent that we love and the partner that we love. All of these things damage our Heart Chakra and our ability to love. Rose quartz helps us to heal and smooth away this damage and enables us to keep on loving with an open heart and an open mind.

Rose Quartz also represents the love between parents and children and can engender balance and harmony in those relationships; very useful if you have a teenager in the house or you have trouble showing your love to your child(ren) or parent(s) for any reason. It is a lovely stone for parents-to-be and for those trying for a child, as it is also said to be a stone of fertility.

It is also representative of the love between friends, for love comes in many varied forms, all of which are amazing. We live quite lonely lives these days compared to our ancestors. Our interactions are less frequent and often more shallow than in times gone by. Finding partners and friends has become a lot more difficult. Rose Quartz and its Faeries work with us to show the universe that we are ready for friendship and love and hint for the universe to introduce us to the right people at the right time.

Rose Quartz can help us take time to heal our hearts after relationships of all kinds fall apart and to see how much we learned from our love and what we can still learn. Rose Quartz heals our emotions, our emotional fears and any issues surrounding love. Rose Quartz lovingly assists us in overcoming abandonment, abuse and lack of love from those who were supposed to love us. It heals heartache and grief, especially those caused by break-ups and loss. This gentle pink stone reminds us all of our great capacity for love and how through love we can heal ourselves and others. It helps us to be more compassionate, more understanding and kinder. It helps us to see and feel things from the points of view of others.

Bringing people together, and establishing meaningful bonds, Rose Quartz harmonises our energies, allowing us to collaborate together through love and with love. This applies to workplaces, communities and families as well as with our romantic partners.

It enables us all to find some common ground, no matter how different we all are, for we all want to be loved. It promotes equality and egalitarianism between us all. It assists us in expressing our true feelings and encourages sharing, especially the sharing of feelings and ideas. Rose Quartz and its Faeries encourage us to seek help when we need it, to allow others to help us and inspire us to help others. Most importantly, Rose Quartz enables us to love and accept ourselves and others for who we are.

Rose Quartz is the stone of all the Faerie monarchs and deities who are linked with love all over the world such as the Chinese Kwan Yin who is also a Goddess of deep compassion, the Roman Venus and Cupid, the Greek Aphrodite, the Aztec Xochipilli, the Egyptian Hathor, the Albanian Prende, the Slavic Živa and the Irish Clíodhna and Oenghus, who fell in love with a girl that he saw in his dreams. Rose Quartz is the stone of the Welsh Faerie Queen Rhiannon who endured many terrible things in the name of love[110], as did Branwen, another Welsh Faerie Queen[111]. Here we see the importance of love in all its forms helping us through tough times and incredible adversities. Rose Quartz is also the stone of both the Norse Goddesses of Love, of Frigg who is the Goddess of Married Love and Marriage, and of Freyja who is the Goddess of Love and Passion. There are so many love deities out there that there is at least one for every type of love imaginable. The Aztec Goddess Xochiquetzal watched over pregnancy and new mothers who were bonding with their babies, Rāgarāja was the Hindu God of Transforming Lust into Spiritual Awareness, Albina was the Etruscan Goddess of Ill-Fated Lovers and Lofn was the Norse Goddess of Forbidden Love.

Rose Quartz and its Faeries want us to love life with a heart brimming over with love. Placing Rose Quartz on your Faerie altar or under the bed while you sleep shows the Faeries that you love them and they will convey their love to you in your magical work, your dreams and even in your everyday life. Rose Quartz gently yet powerfully connects us with the magnificent flow of love that is all around and within us. Opening our hearts and our lives to love, and helping us to truly forgive, Rose Quartz makes it possible for us to discover and re-discover the power and the joy of love.

Rose Quartz nourishes and supports us with its love, enabling us to grow in love and with love, just as good parents, partners and friends do. Calming anger and easing frustrations, it encourages tenderness and sensitivity. It is a very calming and healing stone, bringing serene peace, harmony and inner happiness. Rose Quartz releases negative emotions and transmutes negative energies into positive, loving energies, which it then radiates out to all who need them. If you choose to wear or carry Rose Quartz, try to keep it as close to your Heart Chakra as possible. Rose Quartz fades in bright sunlight, so be careful where you place it.

Smoky/Smokey Quartz

Other Names: Morion when very dark, also known as Cairngorm, when found in the Scottish Highlands and as Colorado Diamond when found in the USA

Chemical Composition: SiO_2 Its smoky colour is from free silicon, formed from the silicon dioxide as a result of natural irradiation

Element: Earth and Deep Earth

Season: Autumn

Planet: Earth

Chakra: Earth Star

Birthstone: Capricorn

Other: National Stone of Scotland

Faerie Monarchs/Deities: Jörð, Nerthus, Danu, Ceridwen, Gaia/Terra, Obair Pheallaidhor/Aberfeldy, Persephone, Rhea, Asherah, Eingana, the Matronae, PachaMama and Mother Earth

Faeries: The Faeries of Scotland, Gnomes, Dwarves, Knockers, Brownies and Brùnaidh

Smoky Quartz ranges in colour from very pale, barely visible champagne hues, through an earthy smoky brown to deep brown to black. In its darkest opaque forms it is called Morion. When mined in Scotland it tends to have quite a yellowy-brown or grey-brown hue and is known as Cairngorm after the mountain range in which it is found. It is used extensively in Scottish jewellery, for kilt pins and for the pommel and handle of the Scottish knife known as the *sgian dubh*.

Smoky Quartz is not only the colour of the ground, but also has the energy of the Earth and soil beneath our feet. It represents the Earth in autumn into which the plants die back and wait below for the renewal of the spring. Smoky Quartz is immensely grounding and stabilising, working with it is like extending your personal roots deep into the soft, nurturing and supportive soil. It grounds and anchors us in the here and now, encouraging realism and practicality in all our endeavours.

An excellent transmuter of negative energies to positive energies, Smoky Quartz eases fear, depression and anxiety. It detoxifies the area around it and can be used to detoxify a room or a person's energies depending on where it is placed and how it is used. Smoky Quartz wishes us to forgive and forget and to leave behind all those things that no longer serve us. Promoting common sense, dependability and credibility, Smoky Quartz is a stone of genuine earthiness. Its grounding influence also allows you to feel settled and more secure.

It is the stone of the pragmatist and all who work with their hands or in a practical way. Smoky Quartz encourages us to hone and develop all of our skills, especially those that are practical, and to look to learn new ones in order to help us to continue to grow. Smoky Quartz assists us in recognising our abilities, our strengths and weaknesses and those of others. Encouraging us to use our rationale and logic, it is a stone of critical thinking and careful discernment. It shows you the value of your experience and reminds you of the valuable advice that you have received and given to others. Teaching you to always act with integrity and to do your research – to literally dig deep – before taking action, Smoky Quartz brings deep understanding, deep knowledge and a deep comprehension of human nature. Smoky Quartz assists us with everything that we do; it is a stone that enables us to plan, prepare and sow our seeds, to then carry out the practicalities, work hard and watch things grow and then, in time, to reap what we have sown. It is a stone of growth and abundance that shows us the importance of nurturing and caring for ourselves so that we too can grow and be enriched.

It is associated with all of the Faeries of the Deep Earth such as the Gnomes, the Knockers who inhabit mines, the Dwarves who work with Mother Earth's mineral wealth and the Brownies who are the Earthy Faeries with whom we share our homes. In particular Cairngorm is linked with the Scottish Brownies, called *Brùnaidh*, whose King is Obair Pheallaidhor/Aberfeldy. With its earthiness, Smoky Quartz is also the stone of all the deities and Faerie monarchs of the Earth, such as the Welsh Ceridwen, the Irish Danu, the Greek Rhea, Gaia and Persephone who lived below in the Deep Earth for the six colder months of the year, the Norse Nerthus and Jörð who gave us our English word 'Earth', the Romano-Celtic Matronae or Mothers, the Sumerian Asherah, the Aboriginal Eingana, the Incan PachaMama and the generic Mother Earth. The Earth and all its deities and Faeries offer us nourishment of the mind, body and soul. If you feel you are suffering from lack, ask for the opportunity to gain what you lack and be prepared to put in the work that they will ask you to do, for it will be provided as an exchange, not simply given – we must reap in order to sow. They encourage us to be generous with what we have so that we can all share this sense of being provided for by our Great Mother. You can call on these monarchs and Faeries for their practical advice at any time.

Work with Smoky Quartz to learn more about your ancestry, your roots and your sense of identity. It shows us how to stand firm and stay true to ourselves, especially during challenging times and with challenging people. Place it beneath the bed or hang it around a bed knob in a little bag if you find yourself getting stressed at night or are suffering with insomnia to take away your worries. Smoky Quartz is the stone of the environmentalist who cares about Mother Earth and the stone of the shaman who journeys the Three Worlds. An ideal companion for lower world journeying, drum work and awakening the soul, it is also great for those who work with animals or animal guides as it has a strong animistic energy. After magical work, journeying or meditation Smoky Quartz eases us gently back to Earth and back into reality. Often used by pregnant women and those who are gestating new ideas or new projects, it has the energy of the soil in which bulbs and seeds gestate before sprouting forth when the time is right. In this same way it is ideal for those undergoing renewal or seeking to renew themselves in any way, for example those looking for a career change, undertaking educational courses, overcoming illness or dis-ease, or those undergoing profound changes in their relationships.

Smokey Quartz keeps it real, encouraging us to be down-to-Earth and unpretentious. Opening and healing our Base and Earth Star Chakras, it keeps both of our feet firmly on the ground and is a great antidote to spaciness. It highlights the need for independence, consolidation and self-sufficiency, encouraging us to get the know the Earth and her seasons by growing our own food and eating what is in season. The smoky colours that give it its name are due to natural irradiation. This is why many crystal healers use Smoky Quartz when working with clients who are going through radiation therapy or have been affected by any form of radiation. It draws off pain, absorbing and transmuting it, teaching us to learn from all of our experiences – even the painful ones.

Snow Quartz

Other Names: Milk Quartz or White Quartz
Chemical Composition: SiO_2 Its white opacity comes from the inclusion of tiny bubbles of liquid, gas, or both
Element: The Snow part of the Ice element and Air
Season: Winter
Planet: The Arctic and Antarctic parts of Earth
Chakra: All Chakras, especially Third Eye, Crown and Soul Star
Birthstone: April
Other: Day Stone for Sundays and Mondays
Faerie Monarchs/Deities: All the snow and winter-associated deities such as Frau Holle, Blizgulis, Snegurochka ('the Snow Maiden'), the Snow Queen, Skadi, Zimarzla and The Cailleach. Also Swanhilde and Caer Ibormeith
Faeries: Whoopers and Swan Maidens, the Huldrefolk, the Sidhe, the Pwca/Puca, the Snow Faeries who create the snowflakes and all Faeries of the far north

Snow Quartz gets its name from the fact that it has the hue and energy of snow. Snow Quartz is a much gentler, calmer form of Quartz than its clear sibling, which encourages deep spiritual serenity and oneness with all things spiritual. It has the tranquillity and beauty of a quiet snow-covered landscape, where beneath the snow nature lies sleeping as it awaits the arrival of spring. Just as nature waits, this stone encourages patience and inner contemplation. If you have trouble switching off from work, or switching off at bedtime, or are experiencing stress, then try holding a Snow Quartz crystal in each hand for a few minutes while contemplating a beautiful snowy scene and let the calmness wash over you and through you. That the opacity of Snow Quartz is due to a multitude of tiny bubbles of air or liquid shows us that sometimes we need to stop and take a breath in order to catch up with ourselves and all that is going on in our lives.

A stone of simplicity and purity, it heals our inner child and restores our sense of wonder, enabling us to see the world in a new way. It is far easier to connect with Faerie energies when we reconnect to our inner child as Faeries are naturally drawn to that energy of innocence. Enhancing our intuition and spiritual awareness, it encourages us to listen to our inner voice and the Divine and the Faeries. Traditionally it has been used to open and heal the Higher Chakras, enabling us to evolve spiritually. Snow Quartz is one of the most Faerie of all stones, for centuries builders refused to use White Quartz in buildings because it was said to be a Faerie Stone and has been utilised at many sacred sites. The great Celtic temple of Newgrange, one of the greatest and grandest constructed Sidhe or Faerie Mounds of all, is surrounded by a facade made from stones of Snow Quartz, which makes it really stand out in the landscape. White Quartz pebbles were used to cover cairns, line pits and even as a kind of flooring for the centre of stone circles as at Druid's Circle at Cefn Coch. Large stones of White Quartz were also used in the construction of several stone circles, such as the eight gleaming Quartz stones of Duloe Stone Circle on Bodmin Moor, the portal stones of Slaney Stone Circle, and several of the Stones of Carrigaphooca in County Cork[112]. Carrigphooca is particularly interesting as its name means 'Rock of the Pwca', a Pwca being a type of Goblin-like Faerie who could be benevolent or malevolent, who often lived near old stone circles and megalithic sites, according to Celtic tales.

Snow Quartz is the stone that is universally loved by all Faeries, especially the northern Faeries and the magical Snow Faeries who create magical and unique snowflakes. These Faeries show us the magic of the world around us and how beautiful our own individuality and uniqueness is. Several snowy characters in Faerie tales are also related to the energies of Snow Quartz, such as Hans Christian Andersen's Snow Queen and *Snegurochka* ('The Snow Maiden') of Russian Faerie tales who seeks human company, but melts when she falls in love. It is also the stone of the many snow deities from the northernmost and southernmost parts of our planet. The Cailleach Beira is the Celtic Queen of Winter who demonstrates the creative power of nature. Skadi is the Norse Goddess of Winter and Snow who shows us to be true to our own nature and to find our own place in this world. Blizgulis is the Lithuanian God of Snow and his name means 'he who shimmers or glitters'; he shows us how to shine forth our inner light. According to Germanic mythology snowflakes are created when the Faerie Queen Frau Holle, or Old Mother Frost as she is also known, shakes the feathers from her bedding. The legend of Frau Holle teaches us the importance of hard work for she rewards her maid who works hard by showering her in Gold, but punishes the lazy maid by covering her with tar! Frau Holle is also the Queen of the *Huldrefolk* – 'The Hidden People'[113] – who are Germanic Mountain Sprites and served by a cheeky race of imps named Hollen after her[114], both of whom adore Snow Quartz.

With its white hue, it is associated with the white feathers of swans, themselves Faerie creatures, and with the Faerie Swan Maidens of Celtic and Norse legend, in particular with Swanhilde, who was the daughter of a mortal woman and a Faerie King, and with Caer Ibormeith, the Celtic Goddess of Sleep and Dreams, who we can ask for help if we are having trouble sleeping or if we wish to have psychic or meaningful dreams. Snow Quartz is very reminiscent of the Whooper Faerie of Sennen Cove that appeared as a white mist that made calls similar to those of the whooper swan to warn locals of any approaching storms.

White stones have long been considered to have healing powers. St Columba had a white healing pebble, probably a Snow Quartz, that he picked up from the banks of the River

Ness. It was placed in water, in which it miraculously floated, and the water was then used to heal all sorts of ailments through the mercy of the Lord[115]. In Carmarthenshire there was a white stone, called the Alluring Stone, that apparently fell from the sky and had the power to cure hydrophobia[116]. Like these other milky hued stones, Snow Quartz is a stone of deep healing. Snow Quartz shows us our need for stillness, solitude and quietness in order to find inner peace and healing. It encourages us to take the time to let ourselves heal, mind body and soul.

Snow Quartz has the freshness of new beginnings and is perfect to keep with you when you are planning or undertaking new projects, starting a new job or new relationship, starting a new course, entering a new phase of life or beginning anything new. It cleanses the Chakras and Aura, restoring harmony and a healthy flow of energy. Snow Quartz demonstrates to us how to be at ease with ourselves and others, and to be honest, diplomatic, accepting, sensitive and tolerant. With its soft white hue, it diffuses and calms difficult situations and calms the emotions and stresses that arise from them. Just like a white flag, White Quartz is symbolic of peace and calling a truce with others when there has been hostility or disagreements. Snow Quartz illustrates our need to be happy with who we are and to find our own happiness in this world. It urges us to find simple yet profound contentment in all areas of our lives.

Part Three: Faerie Quartz Formations

Quartz comes in many forms and many colours; it is one of the most common minerals on Earth. All Quartzes are considered Faerie stones, especially Snow Quartz, which was used to decorate ancient barrows, tombs and other sacred sites including Newgrange in Ireland, itself a Faerie Mound. Several specific forms of Quartz have even earned themselves appropriately Faerie linked names over the years. These crystals may be of any colour, so can be of Amethyst, Clear Quartz, Rose Quartz, Snow Quartz or any other Quartz type.

Elven Star Quartz

Other Names: Master Crystal or Master Channelling Crystal
Chemical Composition: SiO_2
Element: All, especially the Faerie elements of Earth, Air, Fire, Water, Above, Below and Within
Season: Winter
Planet: The seven 'planets' known in the ancient world: the Moon, Mercury, Venus, Sun, Mars, Jupiter and Saturn, especially Saturn as the seventh planet
Chakra: All seven main Chakras: Base, Sacral, Solar Plexus, Heart, Throat, Third Eye and Crown
Faerie Monarchs/Deities: All
Faeries: All

Elven Star Quartz crystals are Quartz crystals where one or more of the facets of the point has seven sides, just as the Elven or Faerie Star has seven points. They are truly magical and make easily accessible gateways to the Realm of the Fae or Otherworld in vision, dream or meditation work.

The seven-pointed star, or heptagram/septagram, is now closely associated with all things Faerie and known as The Faerie or Elven Star. There's a story that mankind was given the five-pointed star as its symbol (although as we shall see later on it also represents the Goddesses and Faerie Queens) because it represents how we view and experience the world – after all we have five senses, while the Fae were given the seven-pointed star to show their very different way of seeing the world. By working with the star of the other race we can each better understand the other. Some believe this Faerie link to the septagram is very ancient indeed, but it seems to have come about (or at least entered popular culture), in the 1980s, courtesy of the Faerie inspired band *The Elf Queen's Daughters*.

No matter how old or how new this connection is, the Elven Star is powerfully symbolic of the Faerie Path and of the Faerie at heart. The Faerie Star acts like a magical pass, reputedly allowing us to safely journey through the Faerie realms or safely work with the Faeries for it shows that we willing and prepared to work with them on their terms. It is a deeply protective symbol and can be carried for protection; many US sheriff's badges show a Faerie Star, including that of the Navajo Tribal Police. Some Faerie workers like to draw the Faerie Star to invoke the protection of the Fae or to use it as a sacred symbol of activation, consecration or blessing. Using a Quartz crystal with a face with seven sides immensely enhances and adds to the power of any Faerie Star that you draw with it. Its uses are limited only by our imaginations, just be sure to use it wisely.

Due to its byname of Master Channelling Crystal, these crystals can also be used to channel messages from the Faeries, allowing their messages for us as individuals and for mankind to come through clearly and comprehensively. Keeping an Elven Star Crystal near you when performing Faerie Card readings will result in a very clear and meaningful reading. If you are channelling the Faeries in other ways, such as writing, painting, or performing, try keeping one of these magical crystals close by to encourage the messages and magic to flow.

Seven has long been considered a very magical and lucky number; in Ancient Egypt it represented eternal life. There are seven orders of angels, seven Hindu sages, seven main Chakras, seven colours in the rainbow and there were seven known planets in the ancient world, which were thought to govern the fate of mankind, depending on when and where we were born, through astrology. The number seven is also of great importance in the area around Glastonbury/Avalon in Somerset, for there are seven sacred springs, seven sacred hills and the labyrinth on Glastonbury Tor has seven tiers. The number seven still guides our lives today as we have seven days in the week.

In Faerie tales and folklore the number seven crops up everywhere you look: the Irish Leprechaun's jacket has seven rows of seven buttons[117], Thomas the Rhymer lived in Faerieland for seven years[118], there are seven Dwarves in the tale of Snow White[119], and in the tales of Oisín he prays for seven days and seven nights and then fights for seven days and seven nights. Another Celtic hero, Cúchulainn, is described as having seven pupils in each eye, seven fingers on each hand and seven toes on each foot[120].

In numerology seven is the number of the magician, the occultist, the psychic and intuitive, the scientist and the thinker. It represents faith, spirituality and enlightenment. Seven signifies completion and mastery of the self, the ego and the elements. Just as the Faerie Star is accessible to mankind to help us comprehend how the Faeries perceive the world, this is the number of understanding, contemplation, thoughtfulness and knowledge.

The pentagram of the human race depicts the five elements: Earth, Air, Fire, Water and Spirit. The septagram of the Elves and Faeries shows seven elements: Earth, Air, Fire, Water, Above, Below and Within. As each point represents a specific element and the colours, Faerie races and monarchs associated with that elements, you can use the Elven Star and Elven Star Quartz as a map of Faerieland and journey around it as you are guided. At each of the points there is a door into a specific elemental Faerie realms and within the centre of the Elven Star or the relevant Facet of the Elven Star Crystal is a direct door that takes you into the very heart of Faerieland.

As with Fairy Wand Quartz, Elven Star Quartz can be used in place of a wand for magical workings, casting circles, delineating space or directing energy/intent. These seven-sided facets can also be a looking glass or door into the world and the workings of the Faeries. Elven Star Quartz acts as a mediator helping the Faeries to understand us humans and helping us humans to understand the Faeries. We are not the same: we have different experiences, different existences, different ways of thinking and working, different missions in life and we live in different worlds that share borders. So if you're experiencing communication or comprehension issues with the Faeries for whatever reason, or that there appears to be something lost in translation, use an Elven Star Quartz to help smooth things through so that you can understand them and they can understand you.

Fairy Castle Quartz

Other Names: Spirit Quartz, Spirit Crystal, Cactus Quartz or Tower Quartz
Chemical Composition: SiO_2
Element: Earth, Spirit, Magic
Season: All
Planet: Earth
Faerie Monarchs/Deities: Arianrhod/Argante, Gwynn ap Nudd and Obair Pheallaidhor/Aberfeldy
Faeries: All household Faeries

Fairy Castle Quartz has the appearance of a Faerie tale castle with a series of crystal points reaching into the sky like turrets. These crystals can be the standard hexagonal Quartz crystals or they may be a rare type of Fairy Spirit Quartz (which we will look at a little later) where the turret or tower crystals are covered with a layer of many smaller sparkly crystals.

They say, *'An Englishman's Home is his Castle.'* Truthfully the same sentiment applies whatever your gender or nationality. The message of Fairy Castle Quartz is all about making our houses into homes and to make room in our homes for our Faerie companions. It does not matter whether your residence is a tiny bedsit or a stately home, for as long as stories have been told we have known that we are not alone in our homes. Every home has at least one Faerie Guardian that will guard our homes, maintain order and harmony, bring good fortune and perhaps perform chores such as sweeping, spinning and helping our bread and cakes to rise, in exchange for board and lodging. Household Faeries are found all over the world and are known by a variety of names: Brùnaidh (Scotland), Brownie (England), Bwbach (Wales), Domovoi (Russia), Dobie (Yorkshire), Fenodyree (Isle of Man), Hob or Lob (Northern England), Jack of the Bowl

(Switzerland), Kobold (Germany), Lares (Ancient Rome), Tomte (Sweden), and Ùruisg/Urisk (Scotland). They may also be of the Green Lady or Glaistig race of Faeries, or if you are in Cornwall there are occasions when a local Pixie has chosen to become a household guardian. Traditionally Household Faeries reside by the hearth or stove, up the chimney, under the stairs, under the threshold or in the centre of the home. Today many houses lack a hearth or stove, so you may find your Household Faerie living by your oven, in your airing cupboard, in a kitchen cupboard or even under a sofa. It is polite to ask your Household Faerie where it is living, so that you can avoid disturbing them too much while your family is going about its daily business.

Household Faeries are really very helpful around the home as long as they are welcome. For the most part they are tied to the house, although there are cases where they have grown so fond of a family that they will move house with them. All types of Household Faeries prefer to live in a well-kept house, one that is generally neat and tidy, for they cannot stand slovenly housekeeping. While they are happy to help out with chores they are not skivvies and hate to be treated as such! In order to stay in their good books, as an acknowledgement of their existence and to show gratitude for their help it is traditional to leave out offerings for the Household Faerie such as bread, cream, milk, porridge or honey. If a Household Faerie is mistreated, ignored or disrespected they can leave to find a place where they will be better treated or they may turn malevolent, perhaps even acting out like a Poltergeist as the Household Faerie at the aptly named *Ty Pwca*, 'House of the Puck/Goblin' in Snowdonia, did after he was insulted.

As with humans, every Household Faerie has their own likes and dislikes. Don't be afraid to ask your Household Faerie(s) what they would like as offerings – it is good manners. Perhaps try holding a Fairy Castle Quartz crystal as you do so to help you to more effectively connect with the Spirit and Faerie of your home. Take note of how well your offerings go down. Listen for their response on the edge of your hearing and pay attention to any feelings you get in your stomach or heart when you leave something out. An offering they like will leave a warm feeling, but one they don't like may give you a niggling, uneasy feeling as you place it out for them. Offerings can be left on special dishes, earthenware dishes are always popular, close to their favourite spot in the house, but be careful to leave it out in a way that will not attract rodents or pests into your home. Offerings do not have to be food, they can be stones or crystals, a picture you have drawn for them and all sorts of things, what's important is your intention behind the gift and that it is appropriate. If we leave something out that is inappropriate or offends them, they may take umbrage and depart as can be seen from these old rhymes:

Pisky [Pixie] fine and Pisky gay,
Pisy's got a bright new coat,
Pisky now will run away.[121]

Give Brownie coat, give Brownie sark [shirt]
Ye'll get nae mair [no more] of Brownie's wark [work]![122]

Don't be surprised if your Household Faerie asks you to leave offerings out in your garden in the form of suitable food for the birds, which the birds then consume. Faeries consume the spirit of the food or gift rather than the physical aspect. There are very strong links between birds, Faeries and some Faerie Monarchs. Robins are the bird of the God Thor and adored by Leprechauns[123] as are magpies (perhaps due to their mutual love of shiny things), house sparrows are beloved by Brownies, crows and all the corvid family are the birds of the Irish Goddess Morríghan[124], the Faerie Queen Morgan le Fay and the Giant Brân the Blessed. Blackbirds are the magical birds of the Welsh Faerie

Queen Rhiannon, owls are the birds of the Goddess Athena/ Minerva (the Latin name for the little owl is *Athene noctua*) and of the God Gwynn ap Nudd (one Mediaeval poet called the owl the *'fowl of Gwyn ap Nudd'*) and many Faeries are said to transform themselves into birds, such as the Hyter Sprites of East Anglia, who fly about in the form of sand martins[125]. Another thing the Household Faerie may ask you do to for them is to plant bug-friendly plants in your garden, if you have one. Again Faeries and butterflies, dragonflies, bees and ladybirds are all close allies; that's why so many Faeries have butterfly or dragonfly-like wings. In Iceland butterflies were sacred to Freyja and known as Freyja's Hens and the *Lady* of ladybird once referred to the Great Goddess and Mother Mary. Fairy Castle Quartz is also associated with the King of the Scottish Brùnaidh, Obair Pheallaidhor/Aberfeldy.

Creating a Faerie altar or Faerie space within your home is a magical experience and welcomes Faerie blessings into your home and your life. It doesn't have to be large or magnificent, it just has to be created with love and light. A shelf or top of a unit makes a great space for an altar. What you place on the altar is up to you, you may like to have something to represent all of the elements, a Faerie Star, crystals that have special meaning to you and the Faeries, your magical tools, Faerie figurines, whatever you like!

There are many ways to make a house more homely, from soft furnishings to candles, and we stamp our personalities on our four walls with our choice of decor and furniture. Our homes are as unique as we are. The important thing is that we feel happy and welcome in our home, just like our Household Faeries. Our homes are a refuge from the world where we live, love, sleep, relax, play, perform our practices, rituals and traditions and simply be ourselves. Homes are magical places and our own Faerie palaces. Fairy Castle Quartz assists in making our homes into our sanctuaries and sacred spaces.

Working with Fairy Castle Quartz in meditation, ritual or even as part of your housework is a truly magical experience. It can be used to assist with spiritual journeying in dream or meditation to the majestic Faerie castles of Gwynn ap Nudd and Argante/Arianrhod, which resemble gigantic, glittering versions of Fairy Castle Quartz. Be sure to always knock first when visiting a Faerie castle, to only enter when permitted and to respect the rules of the castle as you would hope others would respect the rules of your home.

In times past castles were built as protective fortresses to safeguard those who dwelt within or took refuge in their walls, which is why Fairy Castle Quartz acts as a shield protecting your home or sacred space from the constant energetic onslaught from others and from its surroundings, such as the energies of your neighbours, passing cars or power lines. Fairy Castle Quartz demonstrates to us how to set boundaries, to learn to say no, to build up our own spiritual and energetic defences and not be too open to energies that might overwhelm or drain our own. It forms a shield around our homes exactly like the Auric shield that we have around our bodies, protecting our personal energies.

Fairy Cavern Quartz

Chemical Composition: SiO_2
Element: Deep Earth and Magic
Season: Winter
Planet: Earth
Chakra: Earth Star
Faerie Monarchs/Deities: Brân the Blessed, King Arthur, Fionn mac Cumhaill, Ceridwen, Rhiannon, The Dagda, Zeus, Corycia and Nyx
Faeries: All, especially Trows, the Sidhe, Cave Faeries and Nymphs

Fairy Cavern Quartz is form of geode inside of which there are thousands of tiny Druzy crystals so that it appears as if the hollow inside of the geode – the cavern – is thickly coated in sparkling, magical Fairy dust. Geodes are spherical hollow geological structures that occur in certain sedimentary and volcanic rocks. The name comes from the Greek γεώδης – 'earthlike'. They are magical caverns in miniature and as such are perfect for Faeries to either reside in or communicate through.

Fairy Cavern Quartz is great to have in the home or on your Fairy altar to give the Faeries somewhere to play and something to play with – especially if they've a cheeky habit of hiding the shiny things around your home. Fairy Cavern Quartz is wonderful to meditate with as it reminds us of the magic and mysteries that lie deep within each and every one of us and teaches us to look within to find our answers.

Caverns are mysterious places, deep within the Earth, where the light rarely, if ever, reaches. Although they are dark, many caverns are considered oddly comforting and safe for they are like dark wombs within our great Mother Earth. Caverns have provided shelter and refuge for man and animal alike and there are several stunning religious and ritual sites within natural or artificially created caverns such as the **Pharaonic** tombs in the Valley of the Kings and the Cave Cathedral carved within the Mokattam mountain in Egypt. Since the earliest times man has adorned the surfaces of caves with artwork such as the vibrant rock art of the Lascaux Caves in France.

There are many caves in Greece that were and still are sacred to Nymphs such as Melissani Cave, Ossa Cave, Phyle Cave and the most famous, the Corycian Cave of Mount Parnassus, which is named after the Nymph of the springs within the cave, Corycia. Pan, the God of Wild Nature was often worshipped in caves or grottoes such as the one on the north slope of the Acropolis in Athens. The Greek Goddess of the Night, Nyx, lived in a cave, and the mighty Father of the Gods, Zeus, was said to have been born in a cave. However, Greece is not alone as there are Faerie caves all over the world, for example at Kuching in Malaysia, Jiangxi in China, in the Mendips of England, in Kendall County in Texas and Stone County in Missouri. There are also countless caves that are inhabited by Faeries or where Faeries can be heard, such as the Barry Island Sea Cave, where if you listen at certain times, it is said you can hear the hammering of Dwarven smiths and the roaring of their furnaces deep below[126].

In British and Irish Faerielore there are many Bronze Age barrows or hollow hills across the landscape that are homes to various kinds of Faeries. In Orkney, many such hollow hills are called Trowie Knowes for the Trows who live within them. In Ireland the Faeries take their name of *Sidhe* directly from the Gaelic word for 'mound'. There are also reputed to be a separate race of Faeries known specifically as Cave Faeries although others consider this another name for the Sidhe[127]. Many Faerie and mortal kings are reputed to lie not dead, but sleeping under hollow hills such as King Arthur, King David, King Olaf of Norway, Grand Duke Vytautas of Lithuania, the Emperor Charlemagne, Fionn mac Cumhaill and Brân the Blessed.

Caverns and caves are like a womb or the crucible of our mind where things are created. Caves are places of birth, death and rebirth. They are the womb that gives birth to us and the grave that then becomes the womb of rebirth. Mankind has also created his own artificial caves or wombs of rebirth, ancient barrows where the dead were placed resemble caverns and it could be argued that the high domes of Old Churches and Mosques have a cavern-like quality to them. Caves were also places of initiation, another kind of death and rebirth. There is a picture on the Gundestrup Cauldron of a Giant or God dunking a man head first into a cauldron, which is often thought to be a representation of the Cauldron of Rebirth. According to local legends, the Pentre Ifan Burial Chamber in Wales was a site of magical initiation for local druids and was known as the 'Womb or Cauldron of Ceridwen'. To our ancestors the cauldron, like the cave was a womb in which things or people could be placed in order to be transformed. Working with Fairy Cavern Quartz will bring about your own ongoing initiation into the mysteries of the Faeries when the time is right. Cauldrons are also associated with the granting of Faerie blessed bounty. The plentiful Cauldron of the *Dagda* – ' Good God' – was one of the four Faerie treasures of Ireland, from which no company ever went away unsatisfied.

Caverns are places of inspiration, where the inspiration comes from deep within or from the Faerie Underworld or Otherworld. Merlin was reputedly inspired by communing with Faeries who dwelt within Merlin's Cave at Tintagel in Cornwall and one of the Macrimmon Piper's was inspired and taught his tunes by a Faerie Queen who dwelt in Piper's Cave on the Isle of Skye. By working with Fairy Cavern Quartz, we too can access the inspiration of the Fae and be inspired to create wonderful works that will enchant all those who encounter them.

Caves are also considered to be entrances to, or mouths of, the Goddess or the Faerie Otherworld. The Faerie Queen Rhiannon emerged from a cave or hollow hill at Gorsedd Arberth[128] at Beltane, and at certain times of the day or year Faeries can be seen trooping out from such places. Many oracles have resided in caves. Nyx issued oracles as did the head of Brân the Blessed and Mother Shipton, who issued many prophecies, and they also dwelt in caves. If you work with oracles or divination in any way, do keep your divinatory tools close to a Fairy Cavern Geode, or keep one close by as you perform readings to maximise their effectiveness.

Meditating with Cavern Quartz can help us to journey within ourselves or to create a whole new rebirth for ourselves, very handy if we wish to break away from the past and re-invent ourselves. Working with Fairy Cavern Quartz we can find or create new aspects within ourselves, develop new abilities and hone those that we already have. With the help of this Quartz and its Faerie Guardians we can safely explore our inner self, our depths, subconscious and our shadows and will undoubtedly learn much about ourselves. We can access inner parts of ourselves to find and access our inner reserves such as those of strength and stamina.

Fairy Cavern Quartz, like Faerie caves, give us access to hidden realms to work with the Faeries of the Deep Earth such as Dwarves and Cave Faeries. Like the Dwarves we are always forging ahead and forging ourselves and our lives as we create the lives we lead. These sparkling geodes can help us to birth new ideas, new projects and find ourselves new beginnings and remind us of the magic of the Deep Earth and the magic that lies deep within ourselves.

Fairy Diamonds

Other Names: Herkimer Diamond, Herkimer Quartz or the Attunement Stone
Chemical Composition: SiO_2
Element: Ice, Spirit and Magic
Season: Winter
Planet: Neptune and Uranus
Chakra: Crown
Faerie Monarchs/Deities: The High Kings and Queens of Faerie like Titania and Oberon and Finvarra and Oonagh. Also Caer Ibormeith
Faeries: All Faeries who love a bit of sparkle

Fairy Diamonds is a name given to very small Herkimer Diamonds, but the name is a misnomer for these lovely crystals are not Diamonds at all but brilliant double-terminated Quartz crystals with exceptional clarity. These bright crystals were originally discovered in Herkimer County, New York, hence their alternate names. They have similar, yet finer, metaphysical properties to Clear Quartz and similar properties to Diamonds, only not quite so fine. Fairy Diamonds have much to teach us about value and worth, for while they are not technically Diamonds and so do not have the commercial value of Diamonds in terms of energy and spirit they are just as valuable. They have just as much wisdom to share with us as Diamonds do. Value is what we give to something and what something means to us. A simple rock gifted in love can be more valuable than a gemstone given for the sake of it. Fairy Diamonds highlight the need to soul-search and to be on the lookout for the deeper meaning and real motivations behind our actions and those of others.

The intense clarity and hardness of these little stones is down to the fact they cooled and formed incredibly slowly. Due to this Fairy Diamonds are stones that demonstrate great patience and perseverance. They highlight how our impatience and urge to rush about gets us nowhere and stops us from seeing where we are going, but that in taking the time to be patient we can see so much more, and see it far more clearly. In many ways its message is, 'Look where you are going,' as it wishes us to really look before we leap so we can see and make plans for what's coming and where we want to go.

Fairy Diamonds are also known as the Attunement Stone as they can be used to attune oneself with whatever or whoever we desire, as long as it is for our higher good. They can attune us to the energies of the Faeries, to the Earth below us, to the stars above, to higher planes and beings and to the energies of others. They can also help stones attune to each other, especially stones that have very different energies, which makes them very handy for grid work. In group work, communal activities and family or work environments, they can help everyone tune into each other's energies resulting in better co-operation and a more pleasant atmosphere. If used in grids they work to clear negative energies and replace them with pure, clear energies often with a very high vibration, they may also serve to protect from electro-magnetic pollution. Fairy Diamonds also are great crystals for any form of healing work as, when placed between two Chakras, they promote a healthy flow of energy between them.

A stone of knowledge it encourages learning in all its forms and enables us to retain the knowledge that we have gained and in time to wisely pass it on to others. It is an ideal stone for any kinds of teachers and students because it attunes them to each other's energies and teaching/learning style creating a better experience for both. Like Quartz, this is a stone of the wise elder or wise one who has gained a great deal of wisdom and experience through their many incarnations.

These stones have very high vibrations, which is why they are the stones of the high monarchs of Faerie. They will also attract all sorts of sparkle loving Faeries into your life for they are drawn to this stone like moths to a flame. They love to play with its light energy and its energies lift theirs just as they do ours. Fairy Diamonds support us in developing our psychic skills and telepathic abilities, especially when we use those to learn from the Faeries.

Fairy Diamonds are considered very pure stones; they have traditionally been used to cleanse and clear negative energies such as geopathic stress, electromagnetism, stress and negative emotions from people and places with their detoxifying capabilities. They assist and support us in letting go of habits, behaviours and addictions that are harming us and our loved ones, but only if we allow them to do their thing. With their double ends, these are stones of balance, bringing balance and harmony to our lives. They help us to balance our energies, emotions and needs with those of others around us and to find a tenable work/life balance. Keeping our spiritual aims clear and pure, they open up our Crown Chakra and connect us with the light and Spirit of the Universe.

Placed under the pillow at night, these crystals may promote lucid dreaming, intuitive dreams and dream recall, so are linked with the Celtic Goddess of Dreams, Caer Ibormeith. You may find yourself dreaming of Faeries or dreaming through ideas into reality, which have been sent by the Faeries. With their double terminations, Fairy Diamonds allow us in-depth two-way interaction with Faeries, allowing a real sharing of energies, ideas and friendship. Like Clear Quartz, they can amplify and focus energies. Fairy Diamonds have energising, inspiring and enlightening qualities and chase away fatigue. Sensitive souls are naturally drawn to these stones for they help us to crystallise ourselves a harder outer shell or 'thicker skin', which protects us from harsh or negative energies from others by deflecting them away into the light rather than back at the other person.

If you wish to advance further in your work with stones, then this is a crystal that is well worth investing in. It can help attune you to the stone Faeries on a whole new level and if you go into stone or crystal healing professionally, it can help you to tune in to your clients and their needs and then to tune into how you work.

Fairy Dust Quartz

Chemical Composition: SiO_2, plus whatever the 'dust' is composed of
Element: Ice, Spirit and Magic
Planet: None, as this is the Crystal of Star Dust
Chakra: None
Faerie Monarchs/Deities: All that shine or sparkle or are linked to sparkling light such as Argante, Arianrhod, Llew, Brighid and especially Olwen of the White Track
Faeries: All that shine or sparkle, such as 'the Shining Ones' or Sidhe

As the name suggests these Quartz crystals look as if they have been dusted with Fairy Dust. This dusting can either be within the crystal or on its surface as little barnacles of tiny other crystals. The dusting can be white or clear if it's other Quartz crystals, golden if it's Pyrite or silvery if it's Galena. Like anything touched by Fairy Dust, this crystal brings a touch of magic and sparkle to your life.

These crystals challenge us to look at what we are leaving behind in our wake and what kind of Karma we are creating for ourselves. What is the legacy we leave behind us? How do others feel after an encounter with us? It doesn't matter if the encounter lasted a second or a lifetime, what do we leave behind for that person? Do they feel drained, empowered, happy or sad? What effect have we had on the lives of others? Have we helped or hindered? Did we enable or empower them?

Fairy Dust Quartz helps us to realistically evaluate our legacy and Karma and to come up with what it is we would like to leave behind us. How will others remember us to each other? What will we be remembered for after we have departed our mortal existence? Where the Faeries and Faerie Dust Quartz comes in is that they want to help us to leave a whole rainbow of sparkly, glittery love and light Fairy Dust in our wake that leaves others and ourselves very happy indeed. They want us to help spread the healing love and light that is so sorely needed.

This type of Quartz is ruled over by the Celtic Goddess and Faerie Queen Olwen of the White Track. Olwen was the daughter of the Hawthorn Giant, Ysbaddaden. Painfully she knew that her father was fated to die if she should ever marry. In true Celtic Faerie tale style a hero named Culhwch fell in love with Olwen and asked to marry her. He was given a series of incredibly difficult feats to perform which, with help from King Arthur and his knights, he succeeded in. Olwen and Culhwch were wed and Ysbaddaden was killed[129]. Despite the circumstances of their courting and marriage, Culhwch and Olwen do seem to have had their 'happy ever after'. Everywhere Olwen went, white flowers grew in her wake. Her name means 'White Footprint'. The stories differ as to exactly which type of flower these white flowers where, some say lilies, some say trefoils, others say that they are the most Faerie of all flowers, the blooms of the hawthorn. Whatever they were, they were a beautiful reminder that Olwen had passed by and left a little of her magic behind. The legend of Olwen shows us how to read lightly on the planet and, when we go out into nature or visit sacred sites, to remember to, *'Take only photos and memories and to leave only footprints.'*

Human lives can be harsh and filled with despair, anxiety and complications. They are not a bed of roses or hawthorn flowers for that matter either. There are invariably consequences to our actions, some we can predict while others give us nasty surprises. Faerie Dust Quartz wants us to live in a way that encourages positive actions and positive consequences, but even with the best will in the world, things can invariably go wrong or do not go as we had hoped. When that happens Fairy Dust Quartz helps us not to allow other people or difficult situations to dull our sparkle. In particular Olwen teaches us not to let others walk all over us, or to stomp all over the magic that we leave behind us. Instead Fairy Dust Quartz and its Faeries encourage us to learn from what has happened and to keep on going forward with positive intentions. The by-line for these crystals really ought to be, 'Keep calm and sparkle on!'

It is often said, quite rightly, by those who work with Faeries that they cannot stand human falsehoods. This is very true in almost all cases, but there is one exception. When things go bad or get us down, the Faeries can bless us with their magical glamour and illusion magic to help us to 'fake it 'til we make it'. This is very true in situations when it is not appropriate for whatever reason for others to see that we have been hurt by their actions. Some people sadly feed on causing others distress. Positive energy attracts negative energy, that's physics as well as metaphysics unfortunately. Fairy Dust Quartz can work with you to shield you and protect you from these negative energies and people, keeping you positive whatever comes your way. So even if deep down we really don't feel like being all sparkly and sharing a load of love and light all the time, Olwen, the shining Faeries and Fairy Dust Quartz can help us to get on and do it anyway. It encourages us not to give in to the darkness or the negative, but to keep on shining. Even if our light is nothing more than a single tiny ember, it can be tended back to its full luminous glory. By spreading that love and light with others, we also receive some of it too, helping us through the tough times, because whatever comes around goes around.

If you are struggling to feel useful in this world or to find a purpose, meditate with Fairy Dust Quartz to find a way forward. Meditate on which causes speak to you and ways in which you can share your light and love with others. Then take practical steps to find a way for you to make a difference, perhaps with volunteering, doing charity work or changing career. The Faeries want you to know that you can make a difference in a thousand different ways, and you are making a positive difference in this world and will continue to do so as long as there is love and light in your heart. Working with the Faeries and Fairy Dust Quartz will help you to realise that and let that love and light out in a safe way where you are protected from the negativity of others.

Fairy/Mermaid Hair Quartz

Other Names: Angel Hair Quartz, Venus Hair Quartz or Rutilated Quartz

Chemical Composition: SiO_2. The inclusions are Titanium Dioxide (TiO_2)

Element: Spirit and Earth

Season: Summer

Planet: Venus

Chakra: All

Faerie Monarchs/Deities: Niamh of the Golden Hair, Sif, Flidais Foltchaín

Faeries: All, especially Mermaids, the Sidhe, the Elves and the Tylwyth Teg

Fairy or Mermaid Hair Quartz is beautiful to behold with its golden threadlike inclusions running through sparkling Clear Quartz. The name *'rutile'* comes from the Latin word *rutilus* meaning 'red' or 'glowing' and in the ancient world there was a great deal of confusion between the colours red, gold and orange. The golden threads are composed of Titanium Dioxide and do look like golden strands of hair – be it human, Faerie or the hair of a Goddess. The strands look delicate, but being composed of Titanium, they are strong and powerful.

Hair has often been associated with power and fertility. Samson lost his powers and prowess when his hair was cut off by Delilah. Forced cutting of hair is an act of humiliation and punishment that everyone can see; many women who were suspected of collaboration with the Nazis had their hair shaved in the Second World War and many Indigenous peoples have had their hair forcibly shorn in an attempt to take their power and identity from them.

In Norse legend Loki once cut off the long golden hair of

Sif, the wife of Thor and a Goddess of Fertility whose hair was linked to the growth of corn in the fields[130]. Not only was Sif understandably livid, but there was a danger to the fertility of the Earth and so the Dwarves were bidden to create a hairpiece from spun Gold for Sif. The Dwarves did such a great job that the new hairpiece continued to grow just as Sif's real hair once did and so the cereal crops were saved.

Golden hair is often considered a Faerie trait, as is red hair in some parts of the world. The Welsh Faeries known as the *Tylwyth Teg* – 'the Fair Family' have pale skin and golden hair. Those with fair hair were considered somehow related to them and blessed by them as the Tylwyth Teg favoured those with golden locks. There is even tell of how they coveted fair hair so much they tried to steal fair-haired children and women! One Faerie Queen famous for her long locks is Niamh of the Golden Hair, daughter of the Sea God Manannán mac Lir and one of the queens of Tír na nÓg – the Land of Eternal Youth and Beauty. The Irish Faerie Queen of the Wild Wood was known as Flidais *Foltchaín* ('Flidais of the Beautiful Hair') and her hair was linked to the foliage of the forest. Flidais, Sif and Niamh encourage us to celebrate our beauty, no matter how long our hair (or even whether we have any at all) and no matter what colour our hair is. They teach us of the strength and power that we all have within us and how that is part of our personal power and beauty. This beauty is not about exterior prettiness, but the deep, powerful beauty of our soul that shines out from us.

Know that the Faeries look to our souls in deciding whether or not they want to work with us. They look for real beauty in us, such as the love and light in your heart and the magic in your soul. These are the things that really matter and shine forth from us. You can call on the Faeries to guide you to see the world from their perspective so that you too can see the real beauty in others and in the world at large.

The Elves, the Tylwyth Teg, the Mermaids, Flidais, Niamh

and Sif want us to take back our beauty and power from those who have tried to take it from us and to let it shine brightly like a beacon. One old name for the Sidhe of Ireland was 'The Shining Ones' because they let their beauty and Faerie glamour shine forth. We have all heard hurtful comments about the way we look: that we are too skinny, too fat, that our nose is too big or too small, that our lips are too full or thin. Sometimes we've even made those comments about ourselves. All these comments damage us and our self-esteem; they take away our power, just as Delilah took Samson's power little by little, one terrible snip at a time. No matter what size you are, no matter how you look, no matter your age, take back your power and realise that you are incredibly beautiful. Yes, you really are! Remember, those who make ugly comments are only revealing their own issues with their own appearance and their own issues with the beauty, or lack thereof, of their own soul. Know that like the Titanium strands within Fairy Hair Quartz you are incredibly strong as Titanium is a very strong metal indeed and you have the strength to overcome all criticism and the strength to be the beautiful being that you are.

As humans, we have been using rocks and shells to beautify ourselves for thousands of years and we are still doing it today. Not only do we wear gemstones around our necks as necklaces or set in rings on our fingers, many beauty and make-up products also contain ground minerals. The Ancient Egyptians ground up Lapis Lazuli for blue eye shadow, Malachite for green and various Lead Oxides for their kohl. It wasn't just for vanity either, to the Ancient Egyptians beauty was sacred and make-up had magical and medicinal purposes. For example, their kohl, although poisonous for its lead content, reduced incidents of eye infections and reduced the harmful effects of the Sun's glare.

Like the Mermaids who comb their long tresses, we are called upon to take care of our hair, our health and energies as our hair often shows the state of our health. Even the chemicals that we consume end up in our hair and can be tested forensically. The Faeries and Mermaids urge us to take good care of ourselves, in terms of both our inner and outer health. They tell us to watch what we eat, for we are what we eat and remind us to use eco-friendly products on our hair and bodies. Mermaids spend hours taking care of their hair and they enjoy doing so. They do not want us to see washing or combing our hair as a chore but as a valuable bit of personal time when we can indulge ourselves a little, just as they do. We all deserve a little bit of pampering or 'me time' sometimes in order to recharge our batteries and remember who we are.

The fact that our hair grows from within us means that it is an extension of ourselves. Many people swear that they can feel with their hair, in the same was as cats can with their whiskers, and that their hair helps extend their personal power and psychic abilities further out from themselves. Our hair is very much a representation of our inner self; how we wear it, colour it and style it are all ways in which we express ourselves and show our inner selves to the world. In times past hairstyles said much about the culture and status of a person and in many cultures long hair is sacred.

Rutilated Quartz is a wonderful healer of energies, it cleanses and clears the Aura and can dissipate energy blockages. It removes negative energies and thoughts, such as those negative feelings and anxieties that we may have about our appearance, and replaces them with nurturing, positive energies.

Faerie Queene Quartz

Other Names: Isis Quartz or Goddess Quartz
Chemical Composition: SiO_2
Element: All, especially the ancient European and modern
Wiccan elements of Earth, Air, Fire, Water and Spirit
Season: Winter
Planet: Venus
Chakra: Crown Chakra and Heart Chakra
Faerie Monarchs/Deities: All the Faerie Queens, especially
the Queen of Elphame, the Faerie Queene, Venus/
Aphrodite and Titania/Diana

These regal Quartz crystals are named after the famous but
incomplete sixteenth century poem, *The Faerie Queene*, by
Edmund Spenser. They are identified by having one or more
facets on their point that has five sides. The ballad of *The Faerie
Queene* is a very long allegorical poem, that was so loved by a
mortal Queen – Elizabeth I – that she awarded Spenser a pension
for life. In fact one of Elizabeth I's sobriquets was Gloriana, after
the name of the Faerie Queene in Spenser's Ballad. The ballad
is filled with knights, (including a female knight by the name
of Britomart), sorcerers, Nymphs and of course *'That greatest
Glorious Queene of Faerie lond.'*[131] The Faerie Queen has many
names: in Ireland she is Oonagh, in Scotland she is known as
the Queen of Elphame – 'Elf-Home', and most famously she is
Titania in Shakespeare's Midsummer Night's Dream. The name
Titania probably derives from the name of the Roman Goddess
of Hunting and the Moon, Diana, after whom the Romanian
and Portuguese Water Nymphs/Faeries the *Zână* and *Xana*
respectively were also named.

The number five has many mystical and mythological
associations: Gawain from Arthurian legend had a five-pointed

star on his shield, in the ancient Mediterranean world there were thought to be five elements (Earth, Air, Fire, Water and Spirit), in Ancient Asia there were also said to be five elements (Wood, Metal, Fire, Water and Earth) and the Greek Underworld had five rivers. There are also some practical associations with the number five: humans have five senses (which is why the pentagram is considered the star of man), we have five tastes (salty, sweet, spicy, sour and bitter), our bodies have five main systems (circulatory system, digestive system, excretory system, nervous system and respiratory system), and we are sustained by five essential nutrients (carbohydrates, fats, minerals, proteins and vitamins), we have five fingers and five toes, plus the modern working week is five days.

The pentagram is also known as the Star of Venus because the path of the planet Venus as viewed from Earth appears to create a pentagram shape in the sky over time. This happens because Venus goes around the Sun about thirteen times to eight of Earth's orbits. Due to this the pentagram and the number five are linked to the Goddesses and Fairy Queens, in particular the Roman Goddess Venus, for whom the planet is named, and her Greek equivalent, Aphrodite.

Whatever your gender or if you are between genders or gender fluid, these Faerie Queene crystals get us in touch with our 'feminine' sides and amplify feminine and queenly energies. These are traditionally the energies of nurturing, sensuality, creativity, fertility and beauty and can be embraced by all of us. Historically women have been oppressed and discriminated against simply for being women, the Faerie Queens and these crystals can help us to overcome any and all forms of discrimination we face in our lives today and to work through any issues regarding oppression or discrimination from previous lives. Faerie Queens are powerful and so are we! These crystals assist us in tapping into our inner power, whatever our gender. Faerie Queene Quartz can put us directly in contact with the power and presence of the Great Goddess or Faerie Queen, by whatever name we choose to use or that She reveals to us. They can also reveal to us which aspect or face of the Goddess/Faerie Queen or which Goddess/Faerie Queen, depending on how you view Her, is wishing to work with us at any particular time.

It is my firm personal belief that all of us who are drawn to work with Faeries not only have guardian angels, spirit animals and spirits of one of more of our ancestors watching over us, but that we also have one or more Faerie Queens and Kings watching out for us too – although perhaps in a bit more of a, 'What is that human up to now?' kind of way! You may think differently and your ideas are perfectly valid, after all they are based on your experience and intuition. Working with Faerie Queene Quartz and the Faerie Queens you will undoubtedly find yourself drawn to specific ones with whom you share an affinity or from whom you can learn. Over time you may find them going into and out of your life, although you may find one or two being a companion throughout your life, and that is perfectly normal.

The Faerie Monarchs take their positions of power very seriously for they know that they need to unite their peoples, lead them wisely and to protect and take good care of their subjects as well as the lands they rule over. They make excellent guides and leaders, but we must always respect their royal position and their courtly etiquette. It is vital to remember that if a Faerie Monarch takes an interest in guiding you, you will always be considered one of their many subjects. That is a great honour, not a belittlement, and comes with its own duties and responsibilities

In numerology five is the number of nature so Faerie Queene Crystals highlight our need to get out into nature and to connect with the Goddess and Faerie Queen through nature. They urge us to take good care of nature, especially the nature close to us such as our gardens and parks. Five is also the number of the dreamer and the misfit, those who have eclectic tastes and wild imaginations. Faerie Queene Quartz enlivens and awakens our imaginations, which adulthood has attempted to shut down. It connects us to the imagination and the endless possibilities that we had as children. Through imagining and day-dreaming we can start the process of identifying and manifesting our hopes and dreams. Here again we are reminded of our own power to make things happen. We are essentially the kings and queens of our own lives and our own little kingdoms over which we must rule wisely and compassionately.

Fairy Spirit Quartz

Other Names: Spirit Quartz, Spirit Crystal or Cactus Quartz
Chemical Composition: SiO_2
Element: Spirit
Season: Summer and winter
Chakra: Soul Star and Crown Chakra
Faerie Monarchs/Deities: The High and Spiritually Minded Kings and Queens of Faerie, such as Gwynn ap Nudd and Gwenhwyfar/Guinevere
Faeries: All

A beautiful form of Quartz from South Africa, Fairy Quartz is formed when a large crystal is encrusted by a layer of many smaller sparkling crystals, looking as if someone has rolled them in salt or sugar. This form is most common with Amethyst and Clear to Snow Quartz, though it can be found in all of Quartzes many colours. They have a very light, bright almost angelic energy that encourages us to gaze at this beautiful magical world with the sense of awe and wonder that we once had as children.

Clusters of Fairy Spirit Quartz are ideal to have on your Fairy altar or in your home or workplace as they help harmonise our relationships with others, be they Faeries or humans. The same is true if they are used in the centre of a healing group or therapy group. These crystals embody the sentiment of the ancient Sanskrit greeting, still used in India and by Reiki practitioners all over the world today of *Namaste* – 'The Spirit within me acknowledges the Spirit in you.' Fairy Spirit Quartz encourages understanding and love between us all on the level of spirit and soul.

It soothes stress with deep spiritual compassion. Fairy Spirit Quartz is very effective at reducing our anxiety levels and teaching us how to deal with and overcome the stresses of our lives in a way that raises us above the trials and tribulations and enables us to take the high road. Always encouraging us to think outside the box, this is a wonderful crystal for the creative or analytical souls out there.

You can work with Fairy Spirit Quartz for all your spiritual questing and endeavours and it will guide you wisely and lovingly as your spirit evolves through life and lessons learned. They can also guide us as we explore the different spiritual paths that exist, helping us to find our own true path, and to integrate what we have learned and experienced on the way.

As the name suggests, Fairy Spirit Quartz links us to the Faerie Worlds on the level of spirit and to the spirit of ancient Faerie tales, which contain deep spiritual wisdom as well as life lessons. It shows us that we are our own plucky hero or heroine in our own Faerie tale with the power to overcome evil and prevail. We may be lucky enough to find our own 'happy ever after', not necessarily with Prince or Princess Charming, but to find happiness and love in ourselves. We write our own stories and guide our own narrative, do not let anyone else write the story of your life for you.

This is the crystal of the High Kings and Queens of Fairy, those who are more spiritually minded and evolved. In many ways these Faerie Monarchs are also spirits because they are so spiritually evolved that they exist between the realm of Fae and the realm of spirit. Gwynn ap Nudd's name means 'Light' or 'White', 'son of Night/Darkness' and as well as being the King of the Welsh Faeries known as the Tylwyth Teg and the King of *Annwn* – 'The Deep', Gwynn was also a psychopomp who led the Wild Hunt of sprites and spirits that takes the dead and dying back to the Otherworld. He is the king of the dying half of the year, the Holly King aspect of the Green Man. Every year, at May Day, he fights the Summer or Oak King, Gwyrthyr, for the hand of the beautiful Creiddylad (or even Guinevere in some versions)[132]. Today Guinevere is best known as being the wife of King Arthur who fell in love with Lancelot and betrayed her king and husband. However, the older Welsh form of her name, *Gwenhwyfar*, belies her true Faerie and Spirit nature for it means something like 'White Spirit' or 'White Sprite'. Once upon a time Gwenhwyfar was a Faerie Queen and Enchantress of Sovereignty akin to Eriu of Ireland. Originally she was the wife of Gwynn ap Nudd and in some of the older stories Arthur is wed to not one, but three Guineveres[133], perhaps representing the Triple Goddess.

Fairy Spirit Quartz opens our Higher Chakras, most noticeably our Crown and Soul Star Chakras, allowing us to open spiritually to the Divine, the cosmos and to Faerie. It enhances our psychic abilities and our spiritual awareness, raising our vibrations to a new level. It does this by effectively detoxifying our minds, bodies and souls of negativity and negative behaviours that we have gathered in this life and in previous lives. Fairy Spirit Quartz promotes spiritual healing, of both the individual and of groups. It may lead you to a spiritual healing or therapy group as part of its way of assisting you. It supports us through all kinds of healing or therapy work, no matter whether you are the healer or the one being healed. Here it embodies the healing power of spirit, and reminds us that our spirit and spirituality is a healing force. Helping you to develop your higher self and higher abilities, they will also help you to bring the spiritual into your everyday life. When used in conjunction with other stones, Fairy Spirit Quartz will help you connect to their spirit, for they are also beings with spirit(s), and amplify and raise their energies as well as your own.

Fairy Wand Quartz

Chemical Composition: SiO_2
Element: Air, Fire, Spirit and Magic
Season: The eternal summer of Faerieland
Chakra: All
Rune/Ogham: All
Faerie Monarchs/Deities: Math, Gwydion and Hermes/ Mercury
Faeries: All

Just like real Fairy wands, these rare crystals are very small, pretty and delicate. A Fairy Wand crystal is a small termination that grew from the top of a much wider and larger crystal, so that they resemble a slim Rapunzel-type tower or sceptre.

They attune us to higher beings such as angels, Faeries and spirit guides and higher energies such as star energy, serving as conduits. If you often find yourself feeling a little spaced out when working with Faerie or other energies, this crystal does not have the same effect because it connects you to higher energies by bringing and channelling those energies down to you. A stone of channelling it will allow higher beings and Faeries to speak to you and through you. This is ideal if you channel Faerie messages in any way or create works inspired by Faeries. Many musicians and writers have been inspired by Faeries in times past and are still being inspired today. If you're feeling in need of some Faerie inspiration, work with Fairy Wand Quartz and listen to any of the many Faerie inspired musical works out there, such as Weber's *Oberon*, Purcell's *Fairy Queen*, Tchaikovsky's *Dance of the Sugar Plum Fairy*, the *Wast Side Trows Reel* or the *Londonderry Air*[134]. You can also try reading Faerie featuring literature for inspiration or insight, such as Shakespeare's *A Midsummer Night's Dream*, Spenser's *Faerie Queene*, Keats' *La Belle Dame sans*

Merci or *The Eve of St Agnes*, Coleridge's *Songs of the Pixies*, Hans Christian Andersen's *The Elf Mound*, Tolkien's *Lord of the Rings* or any of the many collected Faerie tales from all over the globe. Fairy Wand Quartz is a magical connector of energies, bringing harmony and tranquillity to discord and disharmony. If your energies feel off in any way meditate with Fairy Wand Quartz to focus in on the issue and to rebalance your energies. Just think of it like the Faerie Godmother's magic wand in Cinderella and countless other Faerie tales, with its ability to transform just about any and everything. Fairy Wand Quartz can help us to transform ourselves and to make the most of changes and transformations that are always occurring around us. There's an old story called *Kate Cracknuts* in which the heroine Kate borrows a Faerie wand from a Faerie baby in order to magically heal her sister[135]. I can't help but sense that when we are symbolically gifted with Fairy Wand Quartz crystal it is always essentially being given with the understanding that we are borrowing rather than owning it, meaning that it is a gift to be truly appreciated and cared for.

These rare crystals truly are an embodiment of the Faerie Magic Wand or Sceptre of Faerie Power. As with any magic wand they can be used to focus and project energies or our will, direct spells and energies, to create sacred space by delineating and drawing a magic circle, drawing magical sigils, as drumsticks to beat on a shaman's drum and acting as a bridge between you and other magical beings.

Faerie Wand crystals tend to seek out their new owner when the time is right for they are like official wands or badges of office, showing that you have reached a certain level of personal power and awareness. Magically wands are weapons and amulets of protection so as always we must we wise about how we use this Faerie tool. Be sure that the Faeries will chide you if you use it in an inappropriate way! Magic wands have been used by magicians and shamans since the earliest times: cave paintings depict them; in Ancient Egypt wands were placed with the dead for use in the afterlife and many deities and Faerie Monarchs have carried wands or sceptres representing their power or gifts. Examples include the Welsh Faerie sorcerers Gwydion and Math, who used his wand to test people[136] or transform people into animals and back again[137] or Hermes' caduceus wand or staff, which is still a symbol of healing and medicine today. There's a wonderful Scottish legend about how Brighid wakes nature back to life in spring by touching the Earth and the plants with her birch, or some say hawthorn, wand/staff at Imbolc and how The Cailleach withers nature back to sleep over the winter by touching everything with her blasting wand/staff of blackthorn at Samhain. You can literally use your Fairy Wand Quartz as a wand in its own right or you can use it as a tip to your wand, perhaps crafting the base of the wand from a Faerie-linked tree such as hawthorn or birch. If you use a wooden wand base, be sure not to harm any tree in any way in sourcing it otherwise you and the Faeries will not get off to a good start. It is best to use storm-felled wood if you can and to thank the tree and its resident Dryad for its gift to you with a suitable biodegradable offering.

Fairy Wand Quartz enables us to accept ourselves and others without judging and to overcome any fears we might have about the unknown. It enhances our intuition, our psychic skills and our wisdom so that the unknown becomes the known and the understood. Some Faerie tales are chilling while others are heartening, but they all contain a great deal of wisdom. Fairy Wand Quartz shows us the true meaning of Faerie tales and educates us on the life lessons they contain. In this it also teaches us the lessons of our own Faerie tale – the one we are living.

The wand is also the Spear of the Faerie Sun King Lugh, one of the four Faerie treasures or jewels of Ireland, against which no adversary could win. Wands or staves are a suit of the minor arcana of Tarot and represent fire, ambition, charisma, power, positive changes, creativity and will. In most decks the wands are the suit of fire, but they can also represent air and the intellect. Fairy Wand Quartz is associated with all of the Runes and Ogham letters because they can be used to energetically and magically draw them out. It is also worth noting that the letters of the Ogham are known as staves and that in Mediaeval Iceland certain Runic sigils were called *Galdrastafur* – 'Magical Staves'. Magical sigils and bind Runes or Ogham can be used for many purposes, to protect, to guard against theft or evil spirits, to bring abundance, to connect with Faerie, to open Faerie Hills and just about anything you can think of. Fairy Quartz Wands encourage us to acknowledge and develop our innate magical abilities and to work with Faerie and human magics, such as working with sigils, creating charms and spells, casting Runes, reading Tarot, working with herbs or crystals, etc., all in a safe, supportive way.

Fairy Wand Quartz asks us why we wish to engage with Faerie and the energies of the world around us. It also asks what we want from life and what our ambitions are for all aspects of our lives. It challenges our sense of purpose and direction in life to ensure that we know what we're doing and where we are going. It instils confidence in our own magical abilities, which enables us to better focus and direct all our energies to where they need to be going, not just our magical energies, but our creative energies too. They can give us direction and show us where to go, especially in regards to our careers and professional lives. Fairy Wand Quartz can provide a much-needed pick-me-up if your energy levels are feeling depleted and tap into your self-confidence, allowing you to feel more confident and be more assertive.

Fairy Wand crystals also act like keys to the realm of Faerie and to the great wisdom and magic of the cosmos. Like athames, they can literally cut through any obstacles that might be stopping us from working with or learning from the Fairies. Fairy Wand Quartz will always add power to your magical workings as long as your work is blessed by the Faeries or for the good of all. Meditating with Fairy Wand crystals connects us to all things Faerie and brings us many Faerie blessings and much Faerie good will.

Part Four: The Human Energy System

The Chakras

The idea of Chakras comes to us from Ancient India. Chakra is Sanskrit for 'spinning wheel' and this is essentially what a Chakra is. Chakras draw in energy from the world around us and the type of energy depends on the Chakra. There are literally hundreds of Chakras all over the human body, most of which are referred to as the minor Chakras. When working with stones and Faeries we tend to work with the nine main Chakras, although some people may prefer to stick to the better known seven main Chakras as seven is a Faerie number and the Elven Star has seven points. Each Chakra is said to have certain colours and stones connected with them. Each Chakra is also linked to a physiological system, a sense and specific parts of our anatomy. The spin of the Chakra tells you how healthy it is: a Chakra can be seen as too open (spinning very fast), spinning in a balanced way, or as closed (spinning slowly, sluggishly or even the wrong way).

The Earth Star Chakra

Location: 1½ to 4 feet under the ground
Colour: Earthy browns
Element: Deep Earth
Stones: Flint and Smoky Quartz

This Chakra enables us to release all wastes from Chakras and Auric systems into the ground for transmutation. This is the Chakra where our roots are – the things that connect us to Mother Earth. It contains Earth elements as it nurtures, cleanses and sustains us. This Chakra dictates how grounded and in touch with the real world we are. It is also linked to our genetics and past life experiences.

The Base Chakra

Location: The perineum, the point between the anus and genitals
Colour: Red
Element: Earth
Parts of the Body: Lymphatic system, the reproductive system, our skeletal system including teeth and bones, the prostate gland in men, the bladder and kidneys, and the lower extremities. Also the nose, since it is the organ of the sense of smell
Relates to: Endocrine gland, adrenal glands
Sense: Smell
Stones: Garnet, Carnelian and Red Cork Marble

The Base Chakra relates to our sense of security, trust and our survival instincts. This is our primal, animal, wild Chakra from where our fight, flight or freeze response comes from. It is also our main connection to the world around us. This Chakra relates to our sexuality, sensuality, fertility, creativity, energy, fears and phobias, personal power, strength, willpower, finances, job and home.

The Sacral Chakra

Location: The centre of the abdomen, below the navel
Colour: Orange
Element: Water
Parts of the Body: Reproductive system, sexual organs, lumbar plexus
Endocrine Gland: The Gonads
Sense: Taste, also our appetite
Stones: Carnelian and cognac-coloured Amber

The Sacral Chakra is associated our reproductive and digestive systems, it rules the things that the body needs, and what it enjoys. Enlightenment, creativity, sensitivity, pleasure, enjoyment of life, our sense of trust, aggression levels, ambitions, appetites, our humour and our emotions are also linked to this Chakra.

The Solar Plexus

Location: Solar Plexus, below the breastbone
Colour: Yellow or gold
Element: Fire
Parts of the Body: The muscular system, the skin, the entire digestive system including the large intestine, stomach, liver and other organs and glands in the region of the solar plexus. Also the eyes, as the organs of sight, and the face, representing figuratively the face we show the world
Endocrine Gland: Pancreas
Sense: Eyesight
Stones: Golden Amber and Iron Pyrites

The Solar Plexus Chakra relates to your perceptions of power, control and freedom. Our digestion of food and knowledge, judgement, intellect, attitudes, perfectionism, insecurities, worries, confidence, respect, expressiveness and spontaneity are all linked with this Chakra as is our sense of how happy we are to be ourselves. Despite its lower location, this is also the Chakra of mental activity and it is associated with the level of being we call the personality/ego.

The Heart Chakra

Location: Centre of the chest
Colour: Emerald green
Element: Air and Water

Parts of the Body: Heart and the circulatory system, as well as the lungs and the entire chest area
Endocrine Gland: Thymus gland, controlling the immune system
Sense: Touch
Stones: Aventurine, Moss/Tree Agate, Green Fluorite and Green Connemara Marble

The Heart Chakra relates to love and to relationships with those we hold close. How much we love ourselves and others emerges here. This is the seat of all of our higher emotions and capabilities such as compassion, happiness, unconditional love, kindness, respect, tenderness, empathy and sympathy. In the centre of our being, this Chakra balances the three higher Chakras of the Spiritual and Metaphysical and the three lower Chakras relating to the material and physical. Our sense of balance can be felt here.

The Throat Chakra

Location: Base of the throat
Colour: Sky blue
Element: Water and Spirit
Parts of the Body: Respiratory system, throat, neck, arms and the hands
Sense: Hearing
Endocrine Gland: Thyroid gland
Stones: Aquamarine and Blue Fluorite

The Throat Chakra is where we express ourselves and communicate from, through speech, writing, art, dance and in countless other ways. It also relates to our sense of peace. It is the Chakra of our intense creativity and of our personal truth, which we long to discover and share. Our sense of individuality and originality emerge from this Chakra. Its lesson is to learn to speak our truth, to be honest and to stand up for ourselves.

The Third Eye or Brow Chakra

Location: Centre of the forehead
Colour: Indigo or purple
Element: Spirit
Parts of the Body: Autonomic nervous system, forehead and temples
Endocrine Gland: Pituitary gland
Sense: The sixth sense
Stones: Amethyst and Purple Fluorite

This Chakra is associated with the Spirit, spirituality, wisdom and the subconscious/unconscious. It is the place where our true motivations are found and is the level of consciousness that directs our actions. Our telepathic abilities, visions and intuition are all emerge from this Chakra. From here we see into the depths and into the beyond through our sixth sense or second sight. We are witnesses to the truth and the world around us and it is here that we find our sense of mindfulness.

The Crown Chakra

Location: Top of the head
Colour: White or violet
Parts of the Body: This Chakra is associated with the top of the head, the brain, and the entire nervous system
Endocrine Gland: Pineal gland
Sense: Empathy, the sense beyond our self
Stones: Chevron Amethyst, Moonstone and Snow Quartz

As the Base Chakra relates to our connection with Mother Earth, this Chakra shows our relationship with our Sky Father in Heaven. It represents our connection with our biological father, which becomes the model for our relationship with authority throughout our lives. It's the seat of the soul as it is where our relationship with the Divine is located, as such it is linked with oneness, unity and our sense of belonging. Here we connect to the interconnectedness of everything.

The Soul Star

Location: Six to 12 inches above the head
Colour: Pale clear and silvery
Element: Cosmos
Stones: Clear Quartz and Fairy Diamond

Through this Chakra we gain knowledge of our soul, our life purposes, life tasks and destiny. It is from here that we connect to the stars and the cosmos.

The Auric Field

The Aura is a light-filled egg-shaped energy field that surrounds our physical bodies. It connects to our physical form through our Chakras and radiates out from them. The Auric Field is rather like an onion, with many concentric layers. All our physical, emotional, mental and spiritual functions resonate in and around our physical body in different layers. The layers become less dense the further from our physical form. You know that feeling where someone is in your personal space; well they literally are, for they are within your outer fields of existence. The layers of the human energy field do intermingle and interact though, unlike the onion's skin. There are seven layers to the Auric Field, which exist on three planes: the Spiritual Plane, the Astral Plane and the Physical Plane. The Spiritual Plane consists of the Ketheric Body, the Celestial Body and the Etheric Template. The Astral Plane contains the Astral Body. The Physical Plane includes the Mental Body, Emotional Body and Etheric Body.

Faeries are naturally attracted to our Auras and the state of our Aura tells them a great deal about us, both generally and about how we are feeling at any point in time. Because they can see our issues in our Auras, they are often happy to help us to identify and deal with any issues that they have spotted. Often we are too involved and too close to our own issues and energy problems to clearly see them, whereas the Faeries can see them more objectively. When taking or looking at photographs you may have noticed sparkles, orbs or little Faeries appearing in or around our Auras. If you are lucky you may even see them when working with or photographing your stones too. This is because we are surrounded by Faeries and Nature Spirits for everything around us is alive and filled with energy.

The Physical Plane

The Mental Body

This is associated with our thoughts and mental processes. It extends beyond the emotional body at about 3-8 inches out from the physical form. It's a bright yellow light around the head and shoulders. Thoughts can sometimes be seen as blobs, and the colours of these depend on how the person feels about the thought. Suitable stones for working on your Mental Body include Amber, Carnelian and Iron Pyrites.

The Emotional Body

This links us to our emotions, and its energy converter is the Sacral Chakra. Our emotions come through this level and can be stored here for some time unless we can learn to forgive and forget. This body resembles the physical form, but is less rigid in form. Its colour varies from bright to dark depending on what a person is feeling at the time. Ideal stones for assisting us in keeping our Emotional Body healthy are Rose Quartz and Green Aventurine.

The Etheric Body

The Etheric Body exists somewhere between energy and matter. It has the same appearance as our physical body as it essentially is the design for our physical body. Its colour can vary between grey and pale blue. It emerges from and has its energies regulated by the Base/Root Chakra. The Etheric Body only extends slightly from the physical form. Stones that work well for our Etheric Body include Fluorite, Snow Quartz and Clear Quartz.

The Astral Plane

The Astral Body

The Astral Body has no fixed shape and it filled with swirling colours, although some see it as taking on our human form. It extends 6 inches to 12 inches from the physical form. Its energy converter is the Heart Chakra. The Astral Plane is where, as the name suggests, we connect to the stars, planets and the cosmos. Fairy Diamonds and Clear Quartz are highly compatible with this energy. This is also the part of us that journeys in meditations and dreams.

The Spiritual Plane

The Etheric Template Body

This is the Etheric blueprint for the human body. It is oval in shape and contains all the Chakras and organs in a negative form, just like the negative of 35mm photography film. Our ancestry, DNA, heritage, experiences and sense of self – all the things that have made us who we are – can all be found here. It contains all of our potential and is associated with sacred geometry and the energy lines of the world around us. Preseli Bluestone works very well with this Etheric Body.

The Celestial Body

This is the emotional level of the spiritual plane. The Celestial Body has a beautiful opalescent, angelic light. It is where we experience spiritual ecstasy, spiritual awakening and the experience of unconditional love. It is via this body that we experience intuition and spiritual awareness. Its energy vortex is the Third Eye or Brow Chakra. Ideal stones for this body are Purple Fluorite and Amethyst.

The Ketheric Body

Contains all the Chakras and the structure of the physical body, extends from the body at about 30 inches to 40 inches. Also sometimes called the Causal Body. It is egg-shaped and golden in colour. From here we see the bigger picture and the interconnectedness of all things. Amber is ideal to work with this Etheric Body. Through it we connect to the ascended masters, saints and Faerie Monarchs. From here also comes our sense of knowing ourselves, our being in the right place at the right time and from this level we follow our spiritual path.

Part Five: Meditations

Meditation to Meet a Stone Faerie

Stone Faeries are wonderful beings who can really help us with our work with the natural world and the world of Faerie, they can open the door to Faerieland, to spiritual awakening, assist us in self-healing and self-discovery, and to learn about how to help them and Mother Earth. They are friendly Faeries and great to get to know, whether you are a beginner on the Faerie Path or an experienced Faerie Shaman. This is a simple meditation to help you to meet one of the many, many Stone Faeries out there. It can easily be adapted to indoor or outdoor situations.

You will need a stone, rock or crystal to work with, preferably one that fits into the palm of your hand. After a while you may find that you will not need the physical connection of an actual stone, but it is better to start with one until you've had some practice.

Select the stone by seeing which one you feel drawn to. Which one catches your eye or appears to jump out at you? It can be rough or polished, a plain rock or a semi-precious gemstone, just know that the stone has drawn your attention for a reason – it wants to communicate with you.

It is important before you begin any spiritual/psychic/healing/ meditative work to protect yourself properly, and afterwards is it important that you ground yourself and return to normal.

Protection Exercise

A good method of protection is the bubble technique. Take a few relaxing breaths, slow and deep, until you feel calm and relaxed. Then visualise a pure Divine white light surrounding you, enclosing you in a light bubble that goes all around you at a distance of about 60cm (2ft). If you're working with a specific stone of another colour you can always visualise the light in the same colour as the stone; this can be lovely to do with a rose light for Rose Quartz and a purple light for Amethyst. Remember to see the bubble as completely surrounding you, even over your head and under your feet. Feel the sense of peace, love and the Divine within the bubble, protecting you. State an affirmation or prayer asking your deity, Faerie Monarch, or if you prefer a more general term try Spirit, grant you guidance, wisdom and protection during your work.

The Meditation

Make yourself comfortable and hold your chosen stone in your hands before you, so that you have a physical connection with it. Now, relax your body. Take seven deep, slow breaths, feeling the air move not only through your lungs, but also through your whole body. Slowly become aware of where you are, then, when you are ready, focus on the stone before you.

Experience the stone with all of your senses. Feel it within your hands. Does it feel warm or cool? Is it heavy or light? How does it make you feel inside? Where do you feel your connection with the stone? Do you feel any warmth or buzzing in your body? See its colour and its clarity. What does that colour mean or say to you? Is it opaque or translucent? Does it have markings? Does it have light play or inclusions? How does it feel? What is its texture? Do you hear anything from the stone, perhaps musical notes, whispering or nature sounds? Really feel the stone's presence close to your Aura. Acknowledge this stone as one living being to another. Spend a while doing this.

Become aware of a light within the centre of the stone, perhaps the same colour as the stone, perhaps not. See tiny and beautiful wings form within the light, then see the rest of the form of a little Faerie. Notice her clothes, made of the gifts of nature. Really look at this Faerie, pay attention again to the detail of her, her face, her eyes, her big smile – she is smiling at you! Smile back. See her dance and move around the stone, filling it with love and healing, and having great fun all at once. See how she combines her work with fun? Can you do anything to help yourself do that more often? How can you bring more fun into your life? The Faerie allows you to watch her for a while; she enjoys your company and finds you as beautiful and interesting as you find her.

If you have anything you would like to ask this Faerie, go ahead. She can help you to care for this stone as she is its guardian. The Stone Faerie will let you know how you can help her and which cleansing method or methods she would like to try. She can also tell you how this stone can help you and what it can bring into your life. She can also offer tips on helping you connect with Mother Nature and with other Faeries and the Faerie Realm. She may also offer you tips on learning how to have fun. Take heed of all that she has to say to you.

The Stone Faerie now gives you a little token, unique to you. It could be anything, a button, a seed, some Faerie dust, but whatever it is, it will be relevant to you – perhaps not in an obvious way though!

Show your appreciation to the Faerie, genuinely appreciate what she does, how she cares for her home stone and how beautiful it is. We all like to be appreciated for the good work that we do. Perhaps gift her stone with some cleansing and recharging by her preferred method(s) and keep it on your Faerie altar or on your person as you put her advice to good use in your life.

Grounding Exercise

Stand or sit with your feet firmly on the floor (barefoot if possible). Relax, and see yourself growing roots like a plant. See the roots extending into the ground. Feel the energy work its way up from the Earth, up your legs, up into your torso, along your arms, and up your neck into your head. Feel yourself filling up with the energy. When the energy has filled you up completely see it cascading from the top of your head and your hands, at the same rate that you are taking it up from your roots. You are a fountain of energy. This way you can benefit from the energy, and return it to the Earth.

After a while imagine a white, silvery light above your head – your Soul Star. See rays of energy coming from above into the Soul Star, making it brighter, and a little larger. Visualise this energy then entering your head through the Crown Chakra and coming down your body, and then entering the Earth via your roots. When you are finished, thank the universe, stars, Earth or your Faerie Monarch or deity and withdraw your roots partially from the Earth, after all we are always connected to the Earth. Return to normal. Gently become aware of the room and the everyday once more. Please do not do any strenuous activity, driving, or machinery work until you have eaten and drunk something and feel fully back to normal.

Once you have experience of working with the Faeries of smaller stones and are comfortable communicating with them in this way, you can work your way up to larger stones, boulders, rock formations, standing stones and even entire stone circles.

Chakra Balancing Meditation with Morgan Le Fay

Morgan le Fay is a Faerie Queen linked with the Magical Isle of Avalon – the Isle of Apples. Originally her father was said to be Avallach – King of Avalon. Her name literally means 'Sea Born' and Morgans are Water Sprites in Welsh, Cornish and Breton lore. Her symbol is the apple, an ancient symbol of wellbeing and magic. Morgan is an ancient Faerie Queen, a Welsh/British Goddess who became in myth the sorceress daughter of Gorlois and Ygraine, half-sister sister of King Arthur and student of Merlin. In my experience she is a changeable Queen, changeable like the seas with both light and dark aspects to her personality and this can make her very understanding of the human condition. Her close association with Water and with the apple and her reputation as a great healer mean that she is a great Faerie Queen to call upon for all matters of wellbeing, harmony, balance and for Chakra/energy balancing.

You can perform this meditation as it, simply with visualisation or you can also bring your favourite stones into play, the choice is yours as always. If you choose to work with stones to enhance this meditation, you can use a stone for each Chakra that corresponds with the colour of that Chakra. Here are just a few examples:

Soul Star Chakra: Silvery and transparent stones such as Fairy Diamonds or Clear Quartz

Crown Chakra: White stones such as Snow Quartz or Moonstone

Third Eye/Brow Chakra: Purple stones, for example Amethyst or Fluorite

Throat Chakra: Blue stones such as Aquamarine

Hearth Chakra: Either pink stones such as Rose Quartz or

green stones such as Aventurine and Moss/Tree Agate
Solar Plexus Chakra: Yellow or gold stones such as Amber
Sacral Chakra: Stones that are orange or copper in colour like Carnelian
Base Chakra: Red stones such as Garnet
Earth Star Chakra: Earthy brown stones such as Smoky Quartz and Flint

Before you begin get everything ready, including your stone companions and make sure that they're all charged, happy and healthy. Also remember to charge and cleanse them after you have finished.

Place a stone on or near each of the corresponding Chakras. For practical reasons it is best if you can lie down somewhere comfortable if you choose to use crystals with this exercise.

Protection Exercise

Take a few deep, slow breaths to relax. Visualise a bubble of white light all around you. Become aware of the love of the Divine and of Faerie within the bubble, protecting and caring for you. Ask the Divine, Spirit or Morgan le Fay to grant you guidance, wisdom and protection during your work.

The Meditation

Call on Morgan and ask her to help you to balance your Chakras, these are energy centres that spin like wheels. Become aware of Morgan's presence with you, as woman in green and blue robes with an aura of love and Faerie energy.

Relax your body. Take seven deep, slow breaths, feeling the air move not only through your lungs, but also through your whole body. Before you is a small waterfall that cascades into a pool surrounded by rounded rocks and the most amazing plants you have ever seen. Faeries flit around the plants and dance in the water. Morgan takes your hand and leads you under the waterfall. The water feels soft and gentle as it runs down your skin, like a thousand Faerie kisses.

The water feels cleansing, refreshing and it washes away all your worries. Morgan smiles at you as you realise that this water is clearing and cleansing your Aura, washing away any clouds or darkness and replacing them with bright light, like sparkles on water.

Now allow the water to work on your main seven Chakras. Work from Crown to Base, with the flow of water. Become aware of your Crown Chakra at the crown of your head. Picture the Chakra as a kind of 'wheel' in a pure white colour. Draw in the water's cleansing energy. Picture the wheel starting to spin in a clockwise direction. (You may alternatively like to picture it as a white flower blossoming.) As it is filled with the beautiful energy, feel that energy cleansing, invigorating and balancing that Chakra.

Then allow the water to work its way down to your Third Eye or Brow Chakra, which is located at your brow. Feel it tingle as the energy cleanses and revitalises this Chakra. See the Chakra blossoming in deepest indigo.

When you are ready move down to the Throat Chakra, at the base of your throat, and picture a blossoming flower the colour of Sapphire or the beautiful ocean. Feel refreshed. Feel tension from your shoulders and lungs ebb away.

Now let the energy fill Heart Chakra; picture the Chakra blossom the purest emerald green. Bask in the energy for a while; feel the love of the Divine and the Universe as the Chakra is revitalized.

Move to the next Chakra, the Solar Plexus, this is your upper stomach area, fill this area with beautiful energy and see the Chakra blossom the most beautiful and brightest yellow. Again feel the waterfall's energy doing its work to balance this Chakra, so that it blossoms or shines.

Now let the water's energy move down to your Sacral Chakra,

which is just above the pubic bone. See this as a beautiful bright orange, see the Chakra absorbing the energy and beginning to spin or blossom. Feel that energy cleansing, clearing and balancing this Chakra.

Then allow the waterfall to work downwards to your Base Chakra, again really sense it cleansing this Chakra so that it becomes a rich Ruby red.

Turn your attention again to the waterfall washing over and through your Aura, now clearing any old or stubborn clouds of darkness.

Know that those negative energies washed away from you will be transmuted/made into positive energies. It is polite to offer those now positive energies to Morgan and the Faeries as your thank you.

Now that you are resonating at a higher level of pure light, with Chakras balanced, you can talk with Morgan about any areas of your life you feel need some harmony. Listen to her response. She may give you a gift, an object or words to guide and help you.

When you are ready to cease this meditation you need to partially close your Chakras. Work downwards through your chakras from the Crown to the Base slowly partially closing your Chakras. Do this by seeing the spin slow a little or the flower to partially close – do not close them or stop the spinning entirely, your Chakras still need to process energy for you! Then step out from under the waterfall and out of the pool. Morgan will guide you.

Grounding Exercise

Remove the stones if you worked with any and ground yourself. Stand or sit with your feet firmly on the floor (barefoot if possible). Relax, and see yourself growing roots, like a plant, see the roots extending into the ground. Feel the energy work its way up from the Earth, up your legs, up into your torso, along your arms, and up your neck into your head. Feel yourself filling up with the energy. When the energy has filled you up completely see it cascading from the top of your head and your hands, at the same rate that you are taking it up from your 'roots'. You are a fountain of energy. This way you can benefit from the energy, and return it to the Earth.

After a while imagine a white, silvery light above your head – your Soul Star. See rays of energy coming from above into the Soul Star, making it brighter, and a little larger. Visualise this energy then entering your head through the Crown Chakra and coming down your body, and then entering the Earth via your roots. When you are finished, thank the universe, stars, Earth or your Faerie Monarch or Deity and withdraw your roots partially from the Earth, and return to normal. Gently become aware of the room and the everyday once more. Please do not do any strenuous activity, driving, or machinery work until you have eaten and drunk something and feel fully back to normal.

Leave a suitable, biodegradable offering in your Faerie space or on your Faerie altar.

References

1   Berger J. (1993) *The Sense of Sight*, New York, Vintage International, pp. 8-9

2   Bill Griffiths, B. (1996) *Aspects of Anglo-Saxon Magic*, Little Downham, Anglo-Saxon Books, p. 114

3   Chatterjee, A. (2014) *The Aesthetic Brain: How We Evolved to Desire Beauty and Enjoy Art*, Oxford University Press, p. 154

4   Aubrey Burl, A. (1999) *Great Stone Circles: Fables, Fictions & Facts*, Yale, Yale University Press, p. 11

5   Paice MacLeod, S. (1960) *The Divine Feminine in Ancient Europe: Goddesses, Sacred Women and the Origins of Western Culture*, Jefferson, MacFarland & Co, p. 81

6   Kennedy, J. (1927) *Folklore and Reminiscences of Strathtay and Grandtully*, Perth, Munro Press

7   MacCulloch, E. (1903) *Guernsey Folklore: A Collection of Popular Superstitions, Legendary Tales, Peculiar Customs, Proverbs, Weather Sayings, etc.*, Elliot Stock, pp. 127-8

8   Walcott, M. (1859) *A Guide to the Coast of Sussex*, London, Edward Stanford, p. 177

9   Tongue, R. (1970) *Forgotten Folk-Tales of the English Counties*, London, Routledge & Kegan Paul, p. 27

10   Evans-Wentz, W.Y. (1911) *The Fairy Faith in Celtic Countries*, Glastonbury, The Lost Library, p. 38

11   IBID. p. 179

12   Griffiths, B. (1996) *Aspects of Anglo-Saxon Magic*, Little Downham, Anglo-Saxon Books, p. 114

13   Adamnan, St. & Reeves, W. (1857) *The Life of St. Columba*, Dublin, Dublin University Press, p. 330

14   IBID. p. LXII

15   Proceedings of the Society of Antiquaries of Scotland, Vol. 27, p. 450

16   IBID. p. 451

17 Henderson, L. & Cowan, E.J. (2001) *Scottish Fairy Belief: A History*, East Linton, Tuckwell Press, p. 93

18 Sikes, W. (1880) *British Goblins*. Glastonbury, The Lost Library, p. 84

19 Guest, C. (1997) *The Lady of the Fountain* in *The Mabinogion*, Mineola, New York, Dover Publications, pp. 109-110

20 Shakespeare, W. (2000) *Romeo and Juliet*, Ware, Wordsworth Classics, Act I. Scene 4, Line 54

21 Burl, A. (2000) *The Stone Circles of Britain, Ireland &Brittany*, Yale, Yale University Press, p. 86

22 Reed, R. (2016) *Good Stuff for your Heart & Mind: A Book of Quotes*, R. Reed, p. 376

23 Pollington, S. (2000) *Leechcraft: Early English Charms, Plantlore & Healing*, Little Downham, Anglo-Saxon Books, p. 434

24 Isager, J. (1991) *Pliny on Art and Society: The Elder Pliny's Chapters on the History of Art*, Odense, Denmark, Odense University Press, p. 216

25 Chwalkowski, F. (2016) *Symbols in Arts, Religion and Culture: The Soul of Nature*, Cambridge, Cambridge Scholars, p. 148

26 'The Hávamál', Ragweed Forge 10 March [online]. Available at https://www.ragweedforge.com/havamal.html (accessed 10 March 2017)

27 Smyrnaeus, Q. *The Fall of Troy*, Harvard, Harvard University Press, p. 163

28 John Jamieson, J. (1810) *Jamieson's Etymological Dictionary of the Scottish Language*, Vol. 2, p. 41

29 *Gifford, J. (2006) The Celtic Wisdom of Tree, London, Godsfield Press, p. 146*

30 Gundarsson, K. (2007) *Elves, Wights & Trolls*, New York, Universe, p. 108

31 Lapidge, M. (ed.) (2000), *The Blackwell Encyclopaedia of Anglo-Saxon England*, Oxford, Blackwell, p. 261

32 Paton, L.A. (1903) *Studies in the Fairy Mythology of Arthurian*

Romance, Boston, Ginn, pp. 259-274

33   Rhys, J. (1901) *Celtic Folklore: Welsh and Manx*, Oxford, Oxford University Press

34   W. Bottrell, (1873) *Traditions and Hearthside Stories of West Cornwall*, Vol. II, Penzance, Beare & Son, pp. 67-8

35   Gundarsson, K. (2007) *Elves, Wights & Trolls*, New York, iUniverse, p. 52

36   Sikes, W. (1880) *British Goblins*, Glastonbury, The Lost Library, p. 132

37   *Wolverton, B.C., Douglas,W.L. & Bounds, K. (July 1989) A Study of Interior Landscape Plants for Indoor Air Pollution Abatement (Report) NASA. NASA-TM-108061*

38   Griffiths, B. (1996) *Aspects of Anglo-Saxon Magic*, Little Downham, Anglo-Saxon Books, p. 125

39   Sturluson, S. *Gylfaginning* in *The Prose Edda*, Forgotten Books, p. 34

40   Sturluson, S. *Grímnismál* in *The Poetic Edda*, Forgotten Books, p. 62

41   Gundarsson, K. (2007) *Elves, Wights & Trolls*, New York, iUniverse, p. 108

42   Briggs, K. (2002) *The Fairies in Tradition and Literature*, London, Routledge Classics, p. 98

43   *Northall, G.F. (1892) English Folk-Rhymes, London,* Kegan, Paul, Trench, Trübner & Co. Ltd

44   IBID

45   Ellis Davidson, H.R. *(1964) Gods and Myths of Northern Europe, London, Penguin Books, p. 27*

46   Griffiths, B. (1996) *Aspects of Anglo-Saxon Magic*, Little Downham, Anglo-Saxon Books, p. 114

47   Carrington, C.E., Jackson, J. & Hampden, J. (1919) *'A History of England'*, Cambridge, CUP Archive, p. 3

48   Sibley J.T. (2009) *The Divine Thunderbolt: Missile of the Gods*, XLibris, p. 247

49   'Fun Facts about Virginia's State Parks', Virginia State Parks

10 March [online]. Available at http://www.dcr.virginia. gov/state-parks/fun-facts?rewrite_uri=state_parks/ funfacts (accessed 10 March 2017)

50 Evans-Wentz, W.Y. (1911) *The Fairy Faith in Celtic Countries*, Glastonbury, The Lost Library, p. 38

51 Evans-Wentz, W.Y. (1911) *The Fairy Faith in Celtic Countries*, Glastonbury, The Lost Library, p. 218

52 Guest, C. (1997) *The Dream of Maxen Wledig* in *The Mabinogion*, Mineola, New York, Dover Publications, p. 53

53 Evans-Wentz, W.Y. (1911) *The Fairy Faith in Celtic Countries*, Glastonbury, The Lost Library, p. 220

54 Hartland, E.S. (1890) *English Fairy and Other Folk Tale*, The Walton Scott Pub. Co., Ltd

55 Pollington, S. (2000) *Leechcraft: Early English Charms, Plantlore & Healing*, Little Downham, Anglo-Saxon Books, p. 438

56 Byock, J. L. (1990) *Saga of the Volsungs*, Berkeley, CA, University of California Press

57 Macnamara, N. (1999) *The Leprechaun Companion*, London, Pavillion, p. 32

58 Waring, P. (1978) *The Dictionary of Omens & Superstitions*, London, Treasure Press, p. 219

59 Gundarsson, K. (2007) *Elves, Wights & Trolls*, New York, iUniverse, p. 70

60 Kirk, R. (1893) *The Secret Commonwealth of Elves, Fauns and Fairies*, London, D. Nutt, p. LIX

61 Sturluson, S. *Völuspá* in *The Poetic Edda*, Forgotten Books, p. 18

62 Mackenzie, D.A. (1917) 'Beira, Queen of Winter' in *Wonder Tales from Scottish Myth and Legend*, New York, Frederick A Stokes Co

63 Ross, R. *(2000) Folklore of the Scottish Highlands*, Stroud, Tempus Publishing Ltd. p. 114

64 Burne, C.S. (2003) *Handbook of Folklore*, Whitefish, MT, Kessinger Publishing

65 Paterson, J.M. (1996) *Tree Wisdom: The Definitive Guidebook to the Myth, Folklore and Healing Power of Trees*, London, Thorsons Element (Harper Collins) p. 289

66 Pliny the Elder (1855) *Natural History*, London, Taylor & Francis, Book 22

67 Guest, C. (1997) *Peredur son of Efrawg* in *The Mabinogion*, Mineola, New York, Dover Publications, p. 144

68 Guest, C. (1997) *The Lady of the Fountain* in *The Mabinogion*, Mineola, New York, Dover Publications, pp. 109-110

69 Shelley, P.B. (1994) *Queen Mab; A Philosophical Poem* in *The Selected Poetry and Prose of Shelley*, Ware, Wordsworth Poetry Library, pp. 3-66

70 Sturluson, S. *Gylfaginning* in *The Prose Edda*, Forgotten Books, p. 34

71 Campbell, J.G. (1900) *Superstitions of the Highlands & Islands of Scotland*, Glasgow, J. Maclehose & Sons

72 Brewster, D & Connell, Prof. (1846) *Analysis of the Elie Pyrope or Garnet* in *The London and Edinburgh Philosophical Magazine and Journal of Science*. Vol. 28, p. 152

73 Mackinlay, J.M. (1893) *Folklore of Scottish Lochs and Springs*, Glasgow, William Hodge & Co, pp. 258-60

74 Bruce-Mitford, R. (1978) *Sword from the ship-burial at Sutton Hoo*, British Museum Highlights, pp. 273–310

75 Bauval, R. & Brophy, T. (2013) *Imhotep the African: Architect of the Cosmos*, San Francisco, Disinformation Books

76 Romer, J. (2007) *The Great Pyramid: Ancient Egypt Revisited*, Cambridge, Cambridge University Press, p. 178

77 Caledonian MacBrayne. '13 Haunting Locations on Scotland's West Coast and Islands' 10 March [online]. Available at https://www.calmac.co.uk/blog/13-haunting-locations-scotland (accessed 10 March 2017)

78 Burl, A. (2000) *The Stone Circles of Britain, Ireland & Brittany*, Yale, Yale University Press, p. 259

79 Evans-Wentz, W.Y. (1911) *The Fairy Faith in Celtic Countries*,

Glastonbury, The Lost Library, p. 179

80 Pollington, S. (2000) *Leechcraft: Early English Charms, Plantlore & Healing*, Little Downham, Anglo–Saxon Books, p. 438

81 Henig, M. (1984) *Religion in Roman Britain*, London, B.T. Batsford

82 Pliny the Elder (1855) *Natural History*, London, Taylor & Francis, Chapter 36

83 Bullfinch, T. (2000) *Bulfinch's Greek and Roman Mythology: The Age of Fable*, Mineola, New York, Dover Publications, p. 266

84 Mackenzie, D.A. (1935) *Scottish Folklore and Folk Life – Studies in Race, Culture and Tradition*, London & Glasgow, Blackie and Son

85 Briggs, K. (2002) *The Fairies in Tradition and Literature*, London, Routledge Classics, p. 278

86 Sagan, C. (2002) *Cosmos*, New York, Random House

87 Gregory, I.A. (2013)*The Essential Celtic Folklore Collection*, Book I, Chapter I, eBookIt.com

88 Carmichael, A. (1992) *The New Moon (305)* in *Carmina Gadelica: Hymns & Incantations*, Edinburgh, Floris Books, p. 285

89 Palmer, R. (1992) *The Folklore of Hereford & Worcester*, Little Logaston, Logaston Press, p. 125

90 Speight, H. (1892) *The Craven and North-west Yorkshire Highlands*, London, Elliot Stock, p. 211

91 Whitlock, R. (1974) *The Folklore of Wiltshire*, London, B.T. Batsford, pp. 23-24

92 Gwynn Jones, T. (1930) *Welsh Folklore & Folk-Custom*, London, Trowbridge & Esher: Redwood Burn, p. 70

93 Lethbridge, T.C. (1957) 'The Wandlebury Giants', *Folklore* Vol. 67, No. 4, pp. 193-203

94 Bane, T. (2013) *Encyclopedia of Fairies in World Folklore and Mythology*, Jefferson, MacFarland & Co, p. 221

95   Dunbar, J. (2016) *The Spirit of the Hedgerow*, Stanmore, Local Legend, pp. 18-19

96   Sturluson, S. *Grímnismál* in *The Poetic Edda*, Forgotten Books, pp. 17-18

97   Yarshater, E (ed.) (1983) *The Cambridge History of Iran*, Volume 3, Cambridge University Press, p. 370

98   Barton, J., Bragg, R., Wood, C. & Pretty, J. (eds.) (2016) *Green Exercise: Linking Nature, Health and Wellbeing*, London, Routledge, p. 28

99   Thorpe, B. (1851) *Northern Mythology: Scandinavian Popular Traditions and Superstitions*, Volume 2, London, Edward Lumley, pp. 73-5

100   Bane, T. (2013) Encyclopedia of Fairies in World Folklore and Mythology, Jefferson, MacFarland & Co, p. 221

101   Castleden, R. (1993) *The Making of Stonehenge*, London, Routledge, p. 101

102   Sikes, W. (1880) *British Goblins*, Glastonbury, The Lost Library, p. 371

103   Burl, A. (1999) *Great Stone Circles: Fables, Fictions & Facts*, Yale, Yale University Press, p. 69

104   Mills, S. (2016) *Auditory Archaeology: Understanding Sound and Hearing in the Past*, London, Routledge, pp. 289-90

105   Sikes, W. (1880) *British Goblins*, Glastonbury, The Lost Library, p. 10

106   IBID. pp. 154-5

107   Shakespeare, W. (1993) *As You Like It*, Ware, Wordsworth Classics, Act II, Scene VII.

108   Bullen, A. (2004) *The Language of Flowers*, Norwich, Jarrold Publishing, p. 26

109   Masiola, R. (2014) *Roses and Peonies: Flower Poetics in Western and Eastern Translation*, Mantova, Italy, Universitas Studorum, p. 17

110   Guest, C. (1997) *Pwyll, Prince of Dyved* in *The Mabinogion*, Mineola, New York, Dover Publications, pp. 1-15

111 IBID. Branwen the Daughter of Lir, pp. 16-27

112 Burl, A. (2000) *The Stone Circles of Britain, Ireland & Brittany*, Yale, Yale University Press, p. 262

113 Grimm, J. (2004) *Teutonic Mythology*, Vol. I, Mineola, New York, Dover Phoenix Edition, pp. 271-2.

114 Altmann, A. (2006) *The Seven Swabians & Other German Folktales*, London, Greenwood Publishing, p. 212

115 Georganta, K., Collignon, F. & Millim, A-M. (2009) *The Apothecary's Chest: Magic, Art and Medication*, Cambridge Cambridge Scholars, p. 93

116 Sikes, W. (1880) *British Goblins*, Glastonbury, The Lost Library, pp. 367-8

117 Yeats, W.B. (2004) *The Collected Works of W.B. Yeats Volume IX: Early Articles & Reviews*, New York, Schribner, p. 79

118 Scott, W. (1821) *The Poetical Works of Sir Walter Scott*, Vol. 1, Edinburgh, Archibald Constable & Co., p. 105

119 Grimm J. & W. (1994) *Snow White & Other Fairytales*, Mineola, New York, Dover Publications

120 *Kinsella, T (translator) (1969) The Táin, Oxford, Oxford University Press, pp. 156-158*

121 Evans–Wentz, W.Y. (1911) *The Fairy Faith in Celtic Countries*, Glastonbury, The Lost Library, p. 184

122 Chambers, R. (1841) *Popular Rhymes of Scotland*, Edinburgh, p. 325

123 Macnamara, N. (1999) *The Leprechaun Companion*, London, Pavillion, p. 9

124 O'Rahilly, C. (ed. & trans.) (1976) *Táin Bó Cuailnge* Recension 1, Dublin, Dublin Institute for Advanced Studies, p. 152

125 *Rabuzzi, D.A. (1984) 'In Pursuit of Norfolk's Hyter Sprites', Folklore, Taylor and Francis, 95 (1)*

126 Barber, C. (2016) *Mysterious Wales*, Stroud, Amberley Publishing

127 Wilde, J.F. (1888) *Ancient Legends, Mystic Charms & Superstitions of Ireland*, London, Ward and Downey

128 Guest, C. (1997) *Pwyll, Prince of Dyved* in *The Mabinogion*, Mineola, New York, Dover Publications, p. 5

129 Guest, C. (1997) *Kilhwch [Culhwch] and Olwen* in *The Mabinogion*, Mineola, New York, Dover Publications, pp. 63-93

130 Ellis Davidson, H.R. (1965) *Gods And Myths of Northern Europe*, London, Penguin, p. 84

131 Spenser, E. (2000) *The Faerie Queene*, The Library of Alexandria

132 Guest, C. (1997) *Kilhwch [Culhwch] and Olwen* in *The Mabinogion*, Mineola, New York, Dover Publications, p. 88

133 Bromwich, R. (2006) *Trioedd Ynys Prydein: The Triads of the Island of Britain*, Cardiff: University of Wales Press. No. 56

134 Gallant, C. (2005) *Keats and Romantic Celticism*, Basingstoke, Palgrave MacMillan, p. 158

135 Jacobs, J. (2015) *English Fairy Tales*, BookRix, GmbH & Co, p. 200

136 Guest, C. (1997) *Math the Son of Manthonwy* in *The Mabinogion*, Mineola, New York, Dover Publications, p. 43

137 IBID. p. 42

Bibliography

Allen Paton, L.A. (1903) *Studies in the Fairy Mythology of Arthurian Romance*, Boston, Ginn

Altmann, A. (2006) *The Seven Swabians & Other German Folktales*, London, Greenwood Publishing

Bane, T. (2013) *Encyclopedia of Fairies in World Folklore and Mythology*, Jefferson, MacFarland & Co

Barber, C. (2016) *Mysterious Wales*, Stroud, Amberley Publishing.

Barton, J., Bragg, R., Wood, C., & Pretty, J. (eds.) (2016) *Green Exercise: Linking Nature, Health and Well–being*, London, Routledge

Bauval, R. & Brophy, T. (2013) *Imhotep the African: Architect of the Cosmos*, San Francisco, Disinformation Books

Berger, J. (1993) *The Sense of Sight*, New York, Vintage International

Bottrell, W. (1873) *Traditions and Hearthside Stories of West Cornwall*, Vol. II, Penzance, Beare & Son

Brewster, D. & Connell, Prof. (1846) *Analysis of the Elie Pyrope or Garnet* in *The London and Edinburgh Philosophical Magazine and Journal of Science*, Vol. 28

Broadhurst, P. & Miller, H. (2006) *The Sun & The Serpent*, Launceston, Mythos Press

Briggs, K. (2002) *The Fairies in Tradition and Literature*, London, Routledge Classics

Bromwich. R. (2006) *Trioedd Ynys Prydein: The Triads of the Island of Britain*, Cardiff: University of Wales Press

Bruce-Mitford, R. (1978) *Sword from the Ship-Burial at Sutton Hoo*, British Museum Highlights

Bullen, A. (2004) *The Language of Flowers*, Norwich, Jarrold Publishing

Bullfinch, T. (2000) *Bulfinch's Greek and Roman Mythology: The Age of Fable*, Mineola, New York, Dover Publications

Burl, A. (1999) *Great Stone Circles: Fables, Fictions & Facts*, Yale,

Yale University Press

Burl, A. (2000) *The Stone Circles of Britain, Ireland & Brittany,* Yale, Yale University Press

Burne, C.S. (2003) *Handbook of Folklore,* Whitefish, MT, Kessinger Publishing

Byock, J.L. (1990) *Saga of the Volsungs,* Berkeley, CA, University of California Press

Campbell, J.G. (1900) *Superstitions of the Highlands & Islands of Scotland,* Glasgow, J. Maclehose & Sons

Carmichael, A. (1992) *Carmina Gadelica: Hymns & Incantations,* Edinburgh, Floris Books

Carrington, C.E., Jackson, J. & Hampden, J. (1919) *'A History of England',* Cambridge, CUP Archive

Castleden, R. (1993) *The Making of Stonehenge,* London, Routledge

Chambers, R. (1841) *Popular Rhymes of Scotland,* Edinburgh

Chatterjee, A. (2014) *The Aesthetic Brain: How We Evolved to Desire Beauty and Enjoy Art,* Oxford, Oxford University Press

Chwalkowski, F. (2016) *Symbols in Arts, Religion and Culture: The Soul of Nature,* Cambridge, Cambridge Scholars

Claassens, G. (2002) *Karel ende Elegast,* Amsterdam, Amsterdam University Press

Dunbar, J. (2016) *The Spirit of the Hedgerow,* Stanmore, Local Legend

Ellis *Davidson, H.R. (1964) Gods and Myths of Northern Europe, London, Penguin Books*

Evans-Wentz, W.Y. (1911) *The Fairy Faith in Celtic Countries,* Glastonbury, The Lost Library

Gallant, C. (2005) *Keats and Romantic Celticism,* Basingstoke, Palgrave MacMillan

Georganta, K., Collignon, F. & Millim. A-M. (2009) *The Apothecary's Chest: Magic, Art and Medication,* Cambridge, Cambridge Scholars

Gifford, J. (2006) The Celtic Wisdom of Trees, London, Godsfield Press

Gregory, I.A. (2013) *The Essential Celtic Folklore Collection,* eBookIt.com

Griffiths, B. (1996) *Aspects of Anglo-Saxon Magic*, Little Downham, Anglo-Saxon Books

Grimm, J. (2004) *Teutonic Mythology*, Vol. I, Mineola, New York, Dover Phoenix Edition

Grimm, J. & W. (1994) *Snow White & Other Fairytales*, Mineola, New York, Dover Publications

Guest, C. (1997) *The Mabinogion*, Mineola, New York, Dover Publications

Gundarsson, K. (2007) *Elves, Wights & Trolls*, New York, iUniverse

Gwynn Jones, T. (1930) *Welsh Folklore & Folk-Custom*, Trowbridge & Esher: Redwood Burn

Hartland, E.S. (1890) *English Fairy and Other Folk Tales*, London, The Walton Scott Pub. Co., Ltd

Henderson, L. & Cowan, E. J. (2001) *Scottish Fairy Belief: A History*, East Linton, Tuckwell Press

Henig, M. (1984) *Religion in Roman Britain*, London, B.T. Batsford

Isager, J. (1991) *Pliny on Art and Society: The Elder Pliny's Chapters on the History of Art*, Odense, Denmark, Odense University Press

Jacobs, J. (2015) English Fairy Tales, BookRix, GmbH & Co

Jamieson, J. (1810) *Jamieson's Etymological Dictionary of the Scottish Language*, Vol. 2

Kennedy, J. (1927) *Folklore and Reminiscences of Strathtay and Grandtully*, Perth, Munro Press

Kinsella, T (translator) (1969) The Táin, Oxford, Oxford University Press

Kirk, R. (1893) *The Secret Commonwealth of Elves, Fauns and Fairies*, London, D. Nutt.

Lapidge, M (ed.) (2000), *The Blackwell Encyclopaedia of Anglo-Saxon England*, Oxford, Blackwell

Lethbridge, T.C. (1957) 'The Wandlebury Giants', *Folklore* Vol. 67, No. 4

MacCulloch, E. (1903) *Guernsey Folklore: A Collection of Popular Superstitions, Legendary Tales, Peculiar Customs, Proverbs, Weather Sayings, etc.,* London, Elliot Stock

Mackenzie, D.A. (1917) 'Beira, Queen of Winter' in *Wonder Tales from Scottish Myth and Legend,,* New York, Frederick A Stokes Co

Mackenzie, D.A. (1935) *Scottish Folklore and Folk Life – Studies in Race, Culture and Tradition,* London & Glasgow, *Blackie*

Mackinlay, J.M. (1893) *Folklore of Scottish Lochs and Springs,* Glasgow, William Hodge & Co

MacLeod, S.P. (1960) *The Divine Feminine in Ancient Europe: Goddesses, Sacred Women and the Origins of Western Culture,* Jefferson, MacFarland & Co

Macnamara, N. (1999) *The Leprechaun Companion,* London, Pavillion

Masiola, R. (2014) *Roses and Peonies: Flower Poetics in Western and Eastern Translation,* Mantova, Italy, Universitas Studorum

Mills, S. (2016) *Auditory Archaeology: Understanding Sound and Hearing in the Past,* London, Routledge

Monmouth, G. (1973) *Historia Regum Britanniae* ('History of the Kings of Britain'), London, Penguin Books

Northall, G.F. (1892) English Folk-Rhymes, London, Kegan, Paul, Trench, Trübner & Co. Ltd

O'Rahilly, C. (ed. & trans.) (1976) *Táin Bó Cuailnge,* Recension 1, Dublin, Dublin Institute for Advanced Studies

Palmer, R. (1992) *The Folklore of Hereford & Worcester,* Little Logaston, Logaston Press

Paterson, J.M. (1996) *Tree Wisdom: The Definitive Guidebook to the Myth, Folklore and Healing Power of Trees,* London, Thorsons Element (Harper Collins)

Pliny the Elder (1855) *Natural History,* London, Taylor and Francis

Pollington, S. (2000) *Leechcraft: Early English Charms, Plantlore & Healing,* Little Downham, Anglo-Saxon Books

Rabuzzi, D.A. (1984) 'In Pursuit of Norfolk's Hyter Sprites', Folklore,

Taylor and Francis

Reed, R. (2016) *Good Stuff for your Heart & Mind: A Book of Quotes.* R. Reed

Rhys, J. (1901) *Celtic Folklore: Welsh and Manx*, Oxford, Oxford University Press

Romer, J. (2007) *The Great Pyramid: Ancient Egypt Revisited,* Cambridge, Cambridge University Press

Ross, A. *(2000) Folklore of the Scottish Highlands, Stroud, Tempus Publishing Ltd*

Sagan, C. (2002) *Cosmos*, New York, Random House

Adamnan, St. & Reeves, W. (1857) *The Life of St. Columba*, Dublin, Dublin University Press

Scott, W. (1821) *The Poetical Works of Sir Walter Scott*, Vol. 1, Edinburgh, Archibald Constable & Co

Shakespeare, W. (1993) *As You Like It*, Ware, Wordsworth Classics

Shakespeare, W. (2000) *Romeo and Juliet*, Ware, Wordsworth Classics

Shelley, P.B. (1994) *Queen Mab; A Philosophical Poem* in *The Selected Poetry and Prose of Shelley*, Ware, Wordsworth Poetry Library

Sibley, J.T. (2009) *The Divine Thunderbolt: Missile of the Gods*, XLibris

Sikes, W. (1880) *British Goblins*, Glastonbury, The Lost Library

Smyrnaeus, Q. *The Fall of Troy*, Harvard, Harvard University Press

Speight, H. (1892) *The Craven and North-West Yorkshire Highlands*, London, Elliot Stock

Spenser, E. (2000) *The Faerie Queene*, The Library of Alexandria

Sturluson, S. *The Poetic Edda*, Forgotten Books

Sturluson, S. *The Prose Edda*, Forgotten Books

Thorpe, B. (1851) *Northern Mythology: Scandinavian Popular Traditions and Superstitions*, Volume 2, London, Edward Lumley

Tongue, R. (1970) *Forgotten Folk-Tales of the English Counties*, London, Routledge & Kegan Paul

Walcott, M. (1859) *A Guide to the Coast of Sussex*, London, Edward Stanford

Waring, P. (1978) *The Dictionary of Omens & Superstitions*, London, Treasure Press

Watkins, A. (1922) *Early British Trackways, Moats, Mounds, Camps and Sites*, London, Simpkin, Maeshall, Hamilton, Keny & Co. Ltd

Watkins, A. (1988) *The Old Straight Track: Its Mounds, Beacons, Moats, Sites and Mark Stones*, London, Abacus Books

Whitlock, R. (1974) *The Folklore of Wiltshire*, London, B.T. Batsford

Wilde, J.F. (1888) *Ancient Legends, Mystic Charms & Superstitions of Ireland*, London, Ward and Downey

Wolverton, B.C., Douglas, W.L., & Bounds, K. *(July 1989) A Study of Interior Landscape Plants For Indoor Air Pollution Abatement (Report) NASA. NASA-TM-108061,*

Yarshater, E. (ed.) (1983) *The Cambridge History of Iran*, Volume 3. Cambridge, Cambridge University Press

Yeats, W.B. (2004) *The Collected Works of W.B. Yeats Volume IX: Early Articles & Reviews*, New York, Schribner

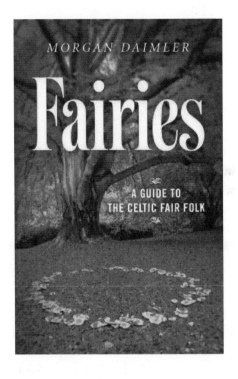

MOON
BOOKS

Moon Books

PAGANISM & SHAMANISM

What is Paganism? A religion, a spirituality, an alternative belief system, nature worship? You can find support for all these definitions (and many more) in dictionaries, encyclopaedias, and text books of religion, but subscribe to any one and the truth will evade you. Above all Paganism is a creative pursuit, an encounter with reality, an exploration of meaning and an expression of the soul. Druids, Heathens, Wiccans and others, all contribute their insights and literary riches to the Pagan tradition. Moon Books invites you to begin or to deepen your own encounter, right here, right now.

If you have enjoyed this book, why not tell other readers by posting a review on your preferred book site. Recent bestsellers from Moon Books are:

Journey to the Dark Goddess
How to Return to Your Soul
Jane Meredith
Discover the powerful secrets of the Dark Goddess and transform your depression, grief and pain into healing and integration.
Paperback: 978-1-84694-677-6 ebook: 978-1-78099-223-5

Shamanic Reiki
Expanded Ways of Working with Universal Life Force Energy
Llyn Roberts, Robert Levy
Shamanism and Reiki are each powerful ways of healing; together,
their power multiplies. Shamanic Reiki introduces techniques to
help healers and Reiki practitioners tap ancient healing wisdom.
Paperback: 978-1-84694-037-8 ebook: 978-1-84694-650-9

Pagan Portals – The Awen Alone
Walking the Path of the Solitary Druid
Joanna van der Hoeven
An introductory guide for the solitary Druid, The Awen Alone
will accompany you as you explore, and seek out your own place
within the natural world.
Paperback: 978-1-78279-547-6 ebook: 978-1-78279-546-9

A Kitchen Witch's World of Magical Herbs & Plants
Rachel Patterson
A journey into the magical world of herbs and plants, filled with
magical uses, folklore, history and practical magic. By popular
writer, blogger and kitchen witch, Tansy Firedragon.
Paperback: 978-1-78279-621-3 ebook: 978-1-78279-620-6

Medicine for the Soul
The Complete Book of Shamanic Healing
Ross Heaven
All you will ever need to know about shamanic healing and how to
become your own shaman...
Paperback: 978-1-78099-419-2 ebook: 978-1-78099-420-8

Shaman Pathways – The Druid Shaman
Exploring the Celtic Otherworld
Danu Forest
A practical guide to Celtic shamanism with exercises and
techniques as well as traditional lore for exploring the Celtic
Otherworld.
Paperback: 978-1-78099-615-8 ebook: 978-1-78099-616-5

Traditional Witchcraft for the Woods and Forests
A Witch's Guide to the Woodland with Guided Meditations and
Pathworking
Melusine Draco
A Witch's guide to walking alone in the woods, with guided
meditations and pathworking.
Paperback: 978-1-84694-803-9 ebook: 978-1-84694-804-6

Wild Earth, Wild Soul
A Manual for an Ecstatic Culture
Bill Pfeiffer
Imagine a nature-based culture so alive and so connected,
spreading like wildfire. This book is the first flame...
Paperback: 978-1-78099-187-0 ebook: 978-1-78099-188-7

Naming the Goddess
Trevor Greenfield
Naming the Goddess is written by over eighty adherents and
scholars of Goddess and Goddess Spirituality.
Paperback: 978-1-78279-476-9 ebook: 978-1-78279-475-2

Shapeshifting into Higher Consciousness
Heal and Transform Yourself and Our World with Ancient
Shamanic and Modern Methods
Llyn Roberts
Ancient and modern methods that you can use every day to transform yourself and make a positive difference in the world.
Paperback: 978-1-84694-843-5 ebook: 978-1-84694-844-2

Readers of ebooks can buy or view any of these bestsellers by clicking on the live link in the title. Most titles are published in paperback and as an ebook. Paperbacks are available in traditional bookshops. Both print and ebook formats are available online.

Find more titles and sign up to our readers' newsletter at
http://www.johnhuntpublishing.com/paganism
Follow us on Facebook at https://www.facebook.com/MoonBooks
and Twitter at https://twitter.com/MoonBooksJHP